BEYOND THREE GENERATIONS

BEYOND THREE GENERATIONS

THE DEFINITIVE GUIDE TO BUILDING ENDURING INDIAN FAMILY BUSINESSES

NAVAS MEERAN | M.S.A. KUMAR | FIROZ MEERAN | GEORGE SKARIA

HARPER BUSINESS

An Imprint of HarperCollins *Publishers*

First published in India by Harper Business 2024
An imprint of HarperCollins *Publishers*
4th Floor, Tower A, Building No. 10, DLF Cyber City,
DLF Phase II, Gurugram, Haryana – 122002
www.harpercollins.co.in

2 4 6 8 10 9 7 5 3 1

P-ISBN: 978-93-5699-835-3
E-ISBN: 978-93-5699-836-0

Typeset in 12/16 Adobe Garamond at
Manipal Technologies Limited, Manipal

Printed and bound at
Thomson Press (India) Ltd

MIX
Paper from responsible sources
FSC® C010615

This book is produced from independently certified FSC® paper to ensure responsible forest management.

To

M.E. Meeran

Founder, Eastern Condiments

Our Beacon of Light

The detailed notes pertaining to this book are available on the HarperCollins *Publishers* India website. Scan this QR code to access the same.

Contents

PREFACE

In 2011, when our father, and founder of the Eastern Condiments Group, M.E. Meeran, passed away, there were many suggestions and requests from our extended family and friends that we—Navas and Firoz—write his biography. But we did not want it to be just the family's perspective; we felt we should bring in an external expert who could add the nuances of institution-building, entrepreneurship and family business management. We had been friends with M.S.A. Kumar for some years then, and we spoke to him about the book. He showed keen interest and, in his own words, shared: 'I was also nearing retirement at the family-owned companies, AVT Natural Products Ltd and AVT McCormick Ingredients Ltd, where I was the non-family professional chief executive officer (CEO).

PREFACE

In 2015, I retired from AVT and completed a course in CEO coaching and Family Business Management at Indian School of Business (ISB), Hyderabad and started advising family businesses in South India. My focus was on small and medium family businesses who needed guidance and direction in their growth and transformation.'

Around the same time, I (Navas) was elected as the Southern Region chairman of the Confederation of Indian Industry (CII) for the year 2014–15. One of my priority tasks at CII was to get more membership from the large industrial belt of Tirupur in Tamil Nadu. A CII delegation went to Tirupur and we discovered that most of the companies there had turnovers between Rs 100 crore and Rs 150 crore, but did not know how to scale beyond that level. The idea of the book became clear then and I, along with M.S.A. Kumar and Firoz, decided to start working on the book.

All three of us had strong ties with the Thomas Schmidheiny Centre for Family Enterprise at Hyderabad led by the renowned Professor Kavil Ramachandran. While discussing the proposed book with him, he suggested that we bring on board New Delhi-based senior journalist George Skaria. All four of us teamed-up in 2021 to work on the book.

George reached out to Ananth Padmanabhan, CEO of HarperCollins India, who introduced us to Sachin Sharma, the vibrant Associate Publisher of HarperCollins India, who has a knack for detecting what appeals to potential readers. In discussion with him, we decided to focus the book as a definitive manual to create enduring Indian family businesses.

As most of us know, various studies across the world have shown that a majority of family businesses do not last beyond three generations. We decided to case-study twelve Indian family businesses that had not only scaled themselves but also demonstrated the potential and promise to create enduring business groups. This book is about the lessons learnt from them.

There are two dimensions to building an enduring family business—business and family. While most books focus on various aspects of family (such as governance, ownership, succession and professionalization), the main focus of this book is on the business dimensions (strategy, positioning, scaling and growing the business, what not to do, and the role of advisors in facilitating transformation and growth). Since family and business are interdependent in family-owned-and-run enterprises, some aspects of family that facilitate the building of a multigenerational enduring family business are also covered.

Gratitude

This book would not have been possible without the collaboration and support of many people. First of all, our gratitude goes to Professor Kavil Ramachandran, who not only reviewed but also agreed to write the foreword to the book.

Our deep thanks go to the business leaders of the eleven other family businesses, who spent considerable time with us sharing their insights and perspectives. These leaders include: Shashank, Virajeet and Gargi at Sandu Pharmaceuticals (Mumbai); Doctors R. Kim and R.D. Thulasiraj at Aravind Eye Care System (Madurai); Kumar Gera of Gera Developments (Pune); George and Jose Ramapuram at Evolve Back (formerly Orange County Resorts & Hotels, Bengaluru); B. Bindumadhav and Abhishek Bindumadhav of Bhima Jewellers (Kochi); Sanjaya Mariwala of OmniActive Health Technologies,

Sanjaya Mariwala Group (Mumbai); V.K. Mathews of IBS Software (Kochi and Singapore); Vanitha and Ramesh Datla of ELICO Ltd (Hyderabad); Mukesh Sawlani, Deepikesh Hira and Yash Dongre of the House of Anita Dongre (Mumbai); John Paul of Popular Automobiles (Kochi) and Sunil Reddy at Dodla Dairy (Hyderabad). We are also grateful to T.V. Sunil, founder at Amicus Capital who shared insights on Chapter 11, 'Unlocking Value and Wealth', noted family business advisors P.M. Kumar and Anil Sainani and family business mediation expert Tara Ollapally who shared their experiences and knowledge.

Jubee Louie Terence, Deepa P.S. and Ajit Joseph from Eastern Condiments and Group Meeran gave us a lot of backend and coordination support. Bengaluru-based Sadhana Sambamoorthy was as usual on top of her work at transcribing the interviews. Our respective families have been with us during the two years that it took us to put this book together and we are grateful to them. Finally, we are very grateful to Ananth Padmanabhan who gave his very early vote of confidence for the concept of the book, which was ably picked up and followed through to its conclusion by HarperCollins India's Associate Publisher, Sachin Sharma. We are also very grateful to Shreya Lall and Sashi Aiyer for helping us with the editing and review of the manuscript and seeing it through completion. The interesting book cover design was done by Saurav Das. Thank you, readers, for your interest in the book and we hope you will find it useful.

—Navas Meeran, Firoz Meeran, M.S.A. Kumar and George Skaria

FOREWORD

THE PAST TWO DECADES HAVE WITNESSED THE emergence of family businesses as an important area of interest to both academics and advisors. Family business owners have increasingly realized that their businesses can grow and successfully transcend generations if they take adequate care to manage the unique challenges that they encounter. Multipronged initiatives taken by the families and other stakeholders have enabled family businesses to be confident in their stride to build successful conglomerates. This is indeed a good beginning, but a lot more needs to be done to accomplish the mission of transformation of family businesses and their sustenance across generations.

It is in this context that I have the opportunity to introduce this book, *Beyond Three Generations: The Definitive Guide to Building Enduring Indian Family Businesses*, coauthored by Navas Meeran, Firoz Meeran, M.S.A. Kumar and George Skaria. While the first two are family business leaders, Kumar is a renowned family business advisor and Skaria, a senior journalist. Obviously, this is the synthesis of the views of four experts, looking at the family business prism from different angles, and the way Indian small- and medium-sized family enterprises (SMEs) have addressed growth and transformation challenges. This book is different from most other books on family businesses! While they, for the most part, discuss challenges and solutions to build family harmony and governance, the focus of this book is on building the business through scaling up operations and addressing growth challenges, while keeping the overall family context in mind. The experiences and lessons learnt are all developed in the family context and explain how the family can be a facilitator or a distractor. This is indeed a unique book from multiple angles.

Conceptually, all organizations undergo major structural changes as they grow from small to medium to large. It is not easy to move into a new and higher orbit that requires not only clarity of the strategy to grow but also a shift in mindset and organizational structure, systems and decision-making processes to follow. Entrepreneurs must learn to work with formal approaches for this journey to be successful. As shown in the diagram that follows, these changes will happen only if the family has good governance practices, including clarity on family's role in the business.

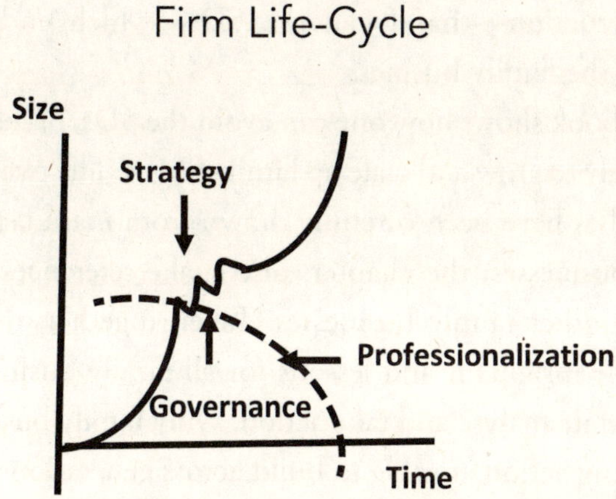

Most family-run SMEs do not anticipate and prepare themselves for this journey of transformation. They remain in the lower growth orbit, often face multiple challenges on both family and business fronts and get trapped in a gridlock. It is useful to remember that one has to keep running, even to remain in the same place, like Alice who was told to run faster to get somewhere ahead.[1]

I like *Beyond Three Generations* because it discusses the growth journeys of twelve Indian large- and medium-sized family businesses that have managed this journey smoothly. They have shown the importance of developing policies and practices to address emerging challenges. As I discussed in my book *The 10 Commandments for Family Business*, a variety of dilemmas crop up especially at the stage of transition to a new orbit.[2] If not prepared well and if not addressed in time, several dilemmas linger on, leading to deviations in thought and action, and if they remain unaddressed, the family business falls into a downward spiral of dilemmas, deviation, differences, disputes and destruction—that I call the 5Ds—which ends with the death of the family business.

This book shows how one can avoid the 5Ds, or address them proactively to grow and scale up family SMEs. The twelve detailed case studies have been carefully drawn from manufacturing and service businesses; the chapters also make references in passing to many other family businesses. Taken together, they provide invaluable insights it and lessons for all family businesses. Read it, discuss it, analyse and take action! Only family businesses that start taking action are able to build across generations.

The beauty of the book lies in its efforts to have a discussion on various overarching themes, such as strategy, professionalization and governance (see exhibit 'Firm Life-Cycle' on the previous page), and weave them all together and share the learning, more like academic research! As noted by the authors, 'Transformation of a family business is not about making a caterpillar crawl faster, but about making it into a beautiful butterfly. And it is this battle between mind and mindset that is necessary for transformation.'

There is increasing realization that family businesses benefit from the services of high-quality advisors, who can not only show a mirror to the family from a neutral angle but also guide them in their journey of transformation. I have always underlined the need to have a large pool of experts that SMEs can draw expertise from. The authors' decision to include a chapter on what advisors can do is another important contribution of the book.

Beyond Three Generations is an excellent source of reference to owners and others interested in family-owned/family-run SMEs. The authors have done a great service by synthesizing the knowledge spread across the chapters and identified seven common features, the 7Cs, that make them unique: clarity, commitment, consistency, courage, cohesion, competency and compounding for scaling-up. It is the synergy created by them all as symphony that makes family SMEs successful. In fact, these 7Cs are critically important for all family businesses, regardless of size, to sustain successfully across generations. Overall, this book has several important and unique features that make it an important contribution to the growing literature on family business.

—Kavil Ramachandran, professor and senior advisor,
Thomas Schmidheiny Centre for Family Enterprise,
Indian School of Business, Hyderabad and Mohali

1

THE ENDURING FAMILY BUSINESS

Beyond Three Generations

FAMILY, AS AN ENTITY, IS ONE OF THE OLDEST SURVIVING institutions of humankind. Yet, family businesses hardly last beyond three generations. One of the main reasons for this unfortunate trend is dilemmas that lead to conflicts in mind and matter under various circumstances. Consider some of these examples in the Indian context:

- A family business owner placed his brother-in-law as the vice president (sales and marketing) of his growing fast moving consumer goods (FMCG) business. Within a year of this decision, he discovered that the incumbent did not have the required expertise to manage the function and grow sales. Torn between a sensitive and delicate family relationship and business responsibilities, the owner was in a dilemma about how to ask his brother-in-law to take up a lesser role or look for another job outside the group. Lack of professionalization and good governance at this juncture would have its impact on the future of the organization.

- In another instance, an eighty-three-year-old family business patriarch, who had built the business from scratch, was reluctant to let go of operational control. He dithered over handing the reins of management to his two sons, who were knocking at his doors. Meanwhile, the business stagnated and missed many opportunities in the marketplace. The patriarch argued that if he did not attend office every day, it would affect his mental health and well-being. Regarding the expansion of the business, till then based in Kerala, the patriarch identified Tamil Nadu as the location for the company's third manufacturing plant. But his dilemma was who would manage the Tamil Nadu factory, since the two sons were running the other two plants based in Kerala. What should the two sons do? Poor succession planning and lack of hiring professionals would have a bearing on the growth of this firm.
- Then we came across this very successful family that wanted to expand and diversify but lacked the internal funds to invest. The patriarch said, 'Let us be happy with what we have', while his son voted for bringing in private equity or venture capital to fund growth. The family business is now at a crossroads. Lack of ambition and the inability to unlock wealth is a serious bottleneck if you want to take the family business to the next generation.

- In another case, to manage growth and transformation, four brothers of a family business felt the need to hand over the reins of leadership to a professional CEO who would report to the family business board. They selected a very competent CEO with a successful track record from the same vertical after a wide search and due diligence. However, the professional CEO quit within six months of joining, citing lack of freedom and space as reasons—a clear case of cultural incompatibility and lack of preparedness of the organization to accept a professional CEO. When a family business grows, unless it is able to bring in and nurture a cadre of professionals, its growth will be stunted.
- Here is another example of two brothers running a large service company with more than 6,000 employees. The younger brother, after attending a family business seminar conducted by renowned South Indian business magazine *Dhanam,* was convinced of the need for a family constitution and a family trust for wealth management. The elder brother disagreed and did not feel the need for the same. Poor governance mechanisms often toll the death knell of family firms.
- A family business owner CEO fell sick and placed her twenty-five-year-old daughter as the executive director (ED) in charge of the business. Two senior vice presidents, each of whom had experience greater than the daughter's age, refused to cooperate. The CEO was left in a dilemma about how to handle the serious situation.
- Again, in a third-generation family business, the granddaughter's compensation was a bone of contention between her grandfather and father. The father wanted to pay

his daughter market-rated compensation commensurate with her qualifications and experience, whereas the grandfather wanted to pay her a token compensation as pocket money. The logic of the patriarch was that as she was part of the family, living with them and not married, she needed to be paid only pocket money. Diversity and equality matter and unless a family firm learns to accept women at leadership and ownership levels on fair terms, the firm and the family may not go very far.

- The management of a leading FMCG company very successfully run by four brothers as a second-generation family business failed to nominate a chairman from among the four to head the family board fearing that choosing one out of the four might create disharmony or even conflict among them. With the third generation entering the business, conflicts emerged on how to run the business. With a leaderless board, differences and disputes became the order of the day. The group was caught on the horns of a dilemma. Could it grow to the next level and the next generation?
- One South Indian business group wanted a family constitution to be written and asked a well-known family business advisor to share a standard template, little realizing that each family business is unique. The family was told that one size does not fit all and that success of a management principle or strategy in one family-managed company does not mean that it can be universally applied with successful results. The group patriarch was also in a quandary on whether to institute a constitution or not. Family constitutions help to avoid conflicts and divisions within a group and are a precursor to growth and longevity.

All of the knotty issues mentioned can and do result in collateral damage to the longevity of family businesses. What starts as a small strain in one generation leads to crises when the business shifts to the next generation. That is why popular and conventional wisdom infers that a majority of family businesses cannot sustain beyond the third generation. It is believed that the genesis of the 'three generations' theory emerged from a 1980s study of manufacturing companies in Illinois.[1] That study is the basis for most of the facts cited about the longevity of family businesses. The researchers took a sample of companies and tried to figure out which of them were still operating during the period they studied. They then grouped the companies into thirty-year blocs, roughly representing generations. Only a third of family businesses in this study made it through the second generation, and only 13 per cent made it through the third.

Professor Kavil Ramachandran recalled an expression, 'shirt sleeves to shirt sleeves', which suggests that the money made by one family generation is exhausted by the time of their grandchildren in the third generation. The same is exemplified in the Brazilian saying 'rich father, noble son, poor grandson'. Many countries have some version of that saying. According to the not-for-profit Parampara Family Business Institute, 'It has been observed that just 13 per cent of family-run businesses survive till the third generation; only 4 per cent go beyond it, and one-third of business families disintegrate because of generational conflict.'[2] Various global studies show that over the decades, 90 per cent of family businesses—even those that manage to scale—do not survive beyond the third, or, maximum, the fourth generation.

Family businesses constitute a majority of the businesses in India and this is the case with most other industrialized nations. Estimates do vary, but the figure is above 75 per cent in all cases.

In the case of the Indian economy, while family businesses constitute about 75 per cent of the economy, 90 per cent of these are believed to be micro, small and medium enterprises (MSMEs). Their importance to the nation cannot be undermined. Together, they contribute about 29 per cent of the country's gross domestic product (GDP) and account for 49 per cent of its exports. It is estimated that the sector has the potential to create ten million new jobs in the next four to five years and be a significant player towards the US$ 5 trillion Indian economy-in-the-making.[3]

Much of the academic and popular literature on family businesses focuses on large groups like the Tatas, Birlas, Ambanis and Mahindras and not on MSMEs. As per the government classification, turnover of MSMEs ranges from an annual Rs 5 crore to Rs 250 crore.[4] Yet, they are not able to dream, scale and grow to the next stage to Rs 1,000 crore and above, due to a variety of crippling challenges. This inability of MSMEs to scale is also a major contributing factor to the death of Indian family MSMEs beyond three generations.

Challenges

In the last three decades since economic liberalization in India, family businesses have gone through a raft of challenges and crises. Rapid expansion in the industrial base has not only created growth opportunities for many, but has also tested their ability to respond to them. In many such cases, families under strain tend to buckle, placing a question mark on their future.

When the Indian economy was opened up in 1991, the majority of the large firms were family-owned. Since the economy was opened up rather suddenly, many family firms that had grown under government protection did not have a strategy ready to respond effectively and experienced the opening up of the economy as a threat rather than an opportunity. These business families went through huge conflicts that sometimes ended with the division of assets.

The difficulty of improving to tackle a competitive environment is made worse by various other factors such as the enhanced need for product knowledge, not knowing how to capitalize on market opportunities, and how to deal with challenging regulatory rules and rapid technology upgradation. Finally, even though a good part of Indian exports comes from the MSMEs, many MSMEs find it difficult to manage in a global environment.

In sum, challenges that inhibit families from growing from generation to generation include:

- limited and strained communication between incumbent and incoming generations;
- inability to handle succession planning;
- lack of attention to issues between division of ownership and management;
- poor understanding of financial issues and lack of financial education for the next generation;

- lack of clarity in terms of devolution, which could lead to insecurity and eventually the breakup of family businesses; and
- complex cross-holding ownership structures that can lead the family into a maze.

Every family is unique and faces unique challenges and situations. Globally companies such as Merck of Germany (thirteen generations over 350 years), and nationally the TVS Group in South India, the Birlas in Kolkata and the Tatas in Mumbai are the stuff of family business folklore.

Sustaining beyond Three Generations: A Roadmap

This book is intended to be a guide to the millions of MSMEs and thousands of larger family businesses on how to build enduring corporations. Written in an anecdotal manner, this book is based on twelve case studies of companies from across the country that are not traditionally large family businesses, but those in a league below them, mostly with turnovers of around Rs 1,000 crore and thereabouts with some exceptions. We tell the story of how they started small, moved into higher leagues and set up processes, systems and a culture to create enduring family businesses that could live beyond three generations.

The companies are well-recognized in their respective sectors and have strong brand equity in regions where they have a market presence. They are: Aravind Eye Care System (Madurai); Bhima Jewellers (Kochi); Dodla Dairy (Hyderabad); Eastern Condiments and Group Meeran (Kochi); ELICO Ltd (Hyderabad); Evolve Back (formerly Orange County Resorts & Hotels; Bengaluru); Gera Developments (Pune); House of Anita Dongre (Mumbai); IBS Software (Kochi and Singapore); OmniActive Health Technologies of the Sanjaya Mariwala Group (Mumbai); Popular Automobiles (Kochi); and Sandu Pharmaceuticals (Mumbai).

From our decades of collective experience in interacting with family businesses and based on our own research, we have identified the ten most critical drivers that will help family business owners and stakeholders to create lasting business groups: mindset; vision and strategy; governance; succession planning; professionalization; building great brands; managing the external environment; going global; unlocking value and wealth; and, the importance of family business advisors.

Expert Take by M.S.A. Kumar

Many books on the management of family businesses are conceptual in nature. However, this book narrates real-life experiences of twelve Indian family-business groups and explores the challenges and promise of building an enduring institution spanning multiple generations. The book draws inspiration from the well-known 5D model of Professor Kavil Ramachandran of ISB, Hyderabad. Starting with the first D (dilemmas), family businesses move through to the last D (destruction), en route having passed through the other three Ds (deviations, differences and disputes). The many examples given at the beginning of this chapter are those that I have encountered in my family business advisory practice. There is no standard prescription that will prevent these dilemmas from leading to destruction, as each family business is unique. Tailor-made prescriptions and solutions have to be administered through continuous dialogue and powerful conversations among family members. When a family overcomes the five Ds, it has built the foundation of an enduring family business.

2

LOOKING BACK

The Roots and the Journey

THE TWELVE CASE STUDIES IN THIS BOOK PRESENT A picture of diversity. While their stories of scale-up have certain unified themes, their beginnings are as diverse as the colours of a rainbow.

Four businesses out of the twelve case studies are wholly or in part in the same or allied field as the original. (i) Aravind Eye Care System emerged from the vision and compassion of Dr Govindappa Venkataswamy (popularly known as Dr V), who established the GOVEL Trust in 1976 and started the first of his not-for-profit institutions, the Aravind Eye Hospital, in Madurai. (ii) Eastern Condiments of Kochi's Group Meeran traces its origins to a humble wholesale grocery store, 'Eastern Coffee and Curry Powder' established in Adimali (about 100 kilometres from Kochi) by M.E. Meeran. (iii) Hyderabad-based ELICO Ltd, India's first analytical instruments firm, owned and managed by the husband–wife team of Ramesh and Vanitha Datla, is an inheritance bestowed by Ramesh Datla's uncle who started the firm in 1960. (iv) Mumbai's Sandu Pharmaceuticals has roots going deep down to an ayurvedic practice started in the 1800s by the forefathers in Rajapur, in Ratnagiri district.

Another two businesses have no connection to any previous business, or businesses. (v) Telangana-based Dodla Dairy led by never-say-die Sunil Dodla Reddy, is the by-product of three previous entrepreneurial failures followed by a gold strike with his fourth enterprise, Dodla Dairy. (vi) IBS Software too is the stand-alone flowering of an idea nurtured by aeronautical engineer V.K. Mathews, which is now flying high.

One business among the twelve, emerged from an up-and-running family business. (vii) Mumbai-headquartered Sanjaya Mariwala's OmniActive Health Technologies is an offshoot of Kancor, the company that Sanjaya headed pre and post the division of the Mariwala family businesses.

The remaining five case studies have either moved into areas far from the original, or have started from the scratch. (viii) Bhima Jewellers, also Kerala-based, owes its origins to Lakshminarayana Bhattar who was born in Udupi, Karnataka, but trudged all the way to the coastal town of Alleppey in Kerala to pursue his school studies and help his uncle in his nondescript restaurant. (ix) The uber-luxury Evolve Back Resorts managed by the seven Ramapuram brothers, has come a long way from the time of its founder—an agriculturist from a well-known Roman Catholic family in the village of Ramapuram, Kerala.

(x) Pritamdas Gera, patriarch of the Gera family, and Kumar Gera of Gera Developments made the difficult journey from Quetta to Pune during the Partition, struggling hard for the family to reach where it has today. (xi) Ultimate in fashion design, the House of Anita Dongre, although synonymous with the high-priestess of fashion, is actually the outcome of collective entrepreneurship among three Mumbai siblings who were raised in a very close-knit family in Bandra. (xii) From washing machines to tyre vulcanizing to becoming one of India's most popular automobile retailing firms, Popular Automobiles owes its existence to the leadership of the fiery erstwhile Communist leader K.P. Paul.

This chapter traces the origins, history and journey of these twelve firms and the families that have dared to dream, scale up and live on the promise of creating enduring family businesses.

Eastern Condiments and Group Meeran: Kochi

In 1950, we became a Republic. Just a year later, even as India was in the throes of the post-Independence nation-building years, young M.E. Meeran, armed with a school education, started a small grocery shop in the unexceptional village of Nellimattom near Kothamangalam in Kerala. From there he hotfooted it about 40 kilometres away, to the scenic and green Adimali more than a decade later in search of better pastures. Adimali is also just 27 kilometres from the famous hill station of Munnar and is home to the Adimali, Cheeyappara and Valara waterfalls. Here, Meeran tried to settle down to a new rhythm of business. Recalls his son Navas, 'My grandfather, Ibrahim, used to borrow money needed from friends and family and give to my father for use in the business. His reputation and credibility were very high.' Meeran would then go to Kochi and parts of Tamil Nadu to source provisions at a cheaper cost.

During his initial days in Adimali, M.E. Meeran observed that sellers used to be known by the name in Malayalam of the trade they were engaged in. Therefore, a betel leaf trader became 'Vettila Shaji', while the man selling iron was called 'Irumbu John'. He wanted a better calling card for himself and a new venture, and zeroed in on Eastern since he had travelled east from his native town. Thus, Eastern Trading Company for the distribution of wholesale provisions was born in 1968. Thereafter, the name Eastern stuck to any future business that he and his sons did.

As his business began to flourish, so did the place and by the 1970s, Adimali had transformed into a busy hub for provisions, with many jeeps queuing on the road for their supply right from the morning. It would not be unfair to say that Meeran was the fulcrum for the growth of trade in Adimali during that period.

For Meeran, Eastern was not just a business but also a means to provide jobs for the underprivileged. Apart from farming jobs, there were hardly any other opportunities in and around the place. Once he set up a full-fledged spice factory and coffee-powder manufacturing facility, Eastern started generating employment. By the 1980s and through the 1990s (Eastern Condiments was incorporated in 1989), hundreds of people lining up for jobs became a common sight in Adimali. Interestingly, the workforce in the factory was dominated by women. It still is. Today, when diversity and equal opportunities are a byword at modern workplaces, it is noteworthy that Meeran was a pioneer practitioner of these concepts.

In the late 1980s the efforts of a few unguided workers of Eastern Coffee and Curry Powder to form a union, goaded by the neighbouring office of a political party, resulted in a strike. Meeran was not in favour of trade unions. He wanted to run his establishment his own way and did not want others to dictate terms to him. The agitation marked the end of Eastern Coffee and Curry Powder and the birth of Eastern Condiments a few kilometres away. He kept the troublemakers away and formed the new company with fresh workers. Needless to say, the agitation fizzled out. Instead of feeling dispirited by the strike, Meeran had seen the green shoots of a new business opportunity. To hedge against such events in the future, he started a second unit in Theni, Tamil Nadu.

Meeran always had the big picture in mind when making a move. One such step, taken in the late 1980s, was to gradually ease out credit given to retail shops. The radical decision proved to be a turning point in the corporate journey of the company, though it went against the normal business practice then. As expected, it didn't go down well with everyone. Nonetheless, Meeran stuck to his guns. 'We need not use all the water flowing in Aluva river to cook rice, we need only enough to cook to satisfy our stomach' was his common refrain. In other words, we should stick to what suits us best instead of dabbling in many things. Meeran also sensed that discount and credit would boost sales temporarily but turn out to be counterproductive in the long run. And he was proved right in later years.

From a small store called 'Eastern Trading Company', the Kochi-based Group Meeran and Eastern Condiments has come a long way with its presence spread across different product verticals and across various countries. Since its inception in 1968 to this day, the group has always innovated for its customers, often anticipating the development of disruptive technologies and innovative ways to meet consumer needs. From tea to technology, treads to mattresses and to affordable homes, Group Meeran is now home to some of the finest brands in the country.

While Meeran laid the foundations of the company, it was his sons Navas and Firoz, who ensured its evolution into a modern enterprise. Navas had become actively involved in the business by the early 1990s, after finishing his college education, Firoz much younger, joined later. After their entry, the company shed much of its traditional garb, embraced multinationals and admitted professionals from outside the family into the organization.

OmniActive Health Technologies: Mumbai

Mention 'Mariwala', and popular recollection jumps to Harsh Mariwala of Marico. Much as that is the harsh reality for Sanjaya Mariwala, the fact is that he too is the architect of a successful family business—OmniActive Health Technologies—in his own right and standing.

Sanjaya Mariwala's career began in 1980 when he joined the family business, Bombay Oil Industries, as a trainee after graduating from Sydenham College, Mumbai. He had the option of going abroad but chose not to. He remembers looking at his career options in terms of what he wanted to do. 'My Dad said why don't you start training in the family business, and see if you like it? If you do, perhaps you can stay on, and get on with life.' The family businesses were run under a flagship company, Bombay Oil Industries Ltd, by Sanjaya's father and his three brothers. 'There was the oils and fats business, there was the industrial chemicals business, and there was the spice and extracts business. Everything was a part of Bombay Oil Industries. It must have been a Rs 40 or Rs 50 crore company at that point of time. Maybe Rs 100 crore at the most,' says Sanjaya.

Sanjaya did a two-year trainee stint, and it was rigorous. He started as a salesman for Parachute Coconut Oil and Saffola, travelling to small towns and cities across India with sales representatives and supervisors. His job involved what he calls 'selling on the street', convincing distributors to pick up the products, and retailers to stock and sell and position the product more effectively to increase visibility. He would be up early at 8 a.m. and soon thereafter waiting outside godowns of distributors, having discussions over chai. 'I travelled by bus, lived in lodges ... it was literally ground-level training.'

Sanjaya recalls that while working as a trainee in Bombay Oil Industries, he realized he enjoyed the work. He consulted some people, 'sort of like mentors or coaches', he says, who helped him figure out the possibility of expanding and growing the business. Post his training period, in 1982, Sanjaya got involved in the family spices and extracts business and was in his early twenties when he was sent to the family's spice extracts plant in Angamali in Kerala, which produced extracts, spice oleoresins, oils and natural colours. At that time, it wasn't doing very well. 'My brief was to go and take a look, develop a business plan, or figure out a way to sell it.' Sanjaya spent a year there and came to the conclusion that it could be turned around. Following his marriage to Nandana in December 1983, the couple moved to Cochin (now Kochi) where they lived for the next twenty-four years.

By the end of the 1980s, Sanjaya (who by now was running the spices extraction business, Kancor) and his cousin Harsh (who ran Marico) realized that they needed to make some changes to the way the family businesses were being run—everything under one company, Bombay Oil Industries. 'Six others from the family, young men, were also going to join the business. We decided that we could not continue to run it the way our parents had. In order to grow, we had to be more professional, and build the management competence needed to expand the business.'

The cousins then took the idea to the elders. It took them some time to be convinced and they had a lot of concerns about changing things. 'We had to bring in a couple of coaches for them too,' says Sanjaya. They brought in two consultants, one was Delhi-based M.B. Athreya. And the other was the Mumbai-based Manish Shrikanth of SP Jain Institute of Management and Research. 'Our elders related to them because of the similar age profile. They were a nice bridge between the youngsters and elders. And a good choice to convince them about the logic of what we were trying to bring to the table.' The consultants gave them the following advice:

- make sure to build consensus about the direction you want to take;
- map out how you will go about meeting the objectives; and
- set very clear goals and objectives in terms of what you are doing, and why.

'I think the "why" was more important than the "what",' says Sanjaya. 'They wanted us to discuss the "whys" at every session to make sure that everyone understood the reasons behind what we were trying to do.' So, the cousins argued how each business was different and needed a different set of skills and management competencies. Pointing to the difference between the Parachute coconut oil and the spice extract business as an example, Sanjaya says, 'We have sales people to sell spice extracts and Parachute coconut oil. Now the coconut oil sales guy runs around the country in a bus. But you can't expect the spice extract salesman to do that. He has to travel abroad, so he would obviously have to fly.'

The various businesses under Bombay Oil were amicably separated by the mid-1990s and Sanjaya remained with Kancor. In 2005, after having led Kancor for twenty-two years, Sanjaya partnered with Hiren Doshi, with the vision to help fill a gap in the market through a customer-centric company, and OmniActive Health Technologies was born. It delivers nature-based ingredients to the evolving natural products industry. Today, OmniActive has global teams in over three continents and 400+ employees to support the key regions. Clearly, in the last eighteen years, Sanjay Mariwala has parachuted himself to the top of the global natural-health products game.

Aravind Eye Care System: Madurai

It is a little over forty-seven years since the farsighted dream of Dr Govindappa Venkataswamy (Dr V) to start an eye hospital to cure all preventable blindness took shape. Post his retirement as an eye surgeon in 1976 at the age of fifty-eight, Dr V established the GOVEL Trust, under which Aravind Eye Hospitals were founded. The first Aravind Eye Hospital was founded by converting the premises of a rented family home into an eleven-bedded hospital with no capital or business plan. The conglomerate Aravind Eye Care System has emerged from that start, with just four medical officers led by Dr V. Today they have a 6,000-strong workforce, including about thirty-five members from the founder's family.

A rare instance of a family non-profit institution, Aravind is also distinctly different from family-involved non-profit foundation-run institutions in the modern world, such as the Bill and Melinda Gates Foundation or the Wipro Foundation of the Premji family, which are funded by corporate profits. Seeking no donations for its core care-giving activities from private, government or foreign funding, it has not been an easy journey.

But then Dr V is a person who has turned the impossible into the possible, having personally performed over 1,00,000 sight-restoring surgeries despite his fingers being crippled due to rheumatoid arthritis. The institution draws its name from spiritual leader Sri Aurobindo and is inspired in all their work by Sri Aurobindo and Mother.

There are a few key milestones and strategies to Aravind's magical journey of growth. First, it developed a human resource (HR) pipeline, especially for support staff. There were no ophthalmic nurses at the beginning of their journey, and general nurses did not have the required expertise in the eye-care field. They started small, by appointing a tutor. Today, they have something akin to a college for basic ophthalmic training. 'Each year, we take in 600 to 800 rural girls, train and employ them,' says R.D. Thulasiraj, ED, operations. 'That has become a major initiative.' Over the years, Aravind has also developed similar HR pipelines for doctors and managers.

In the late 1980s, technology changed for the implant of an intraocular lens following the removal of cataracts. However, the World Health Organization (WHO), along with most governments in developing countries, was against it because it was (due to the cost of the lens then) a very expensive surgery and required highly skilled personnel. Other eye-care related medical innovations had also come in—scans to determine power, microscopes for doing surgery, and more. But these innovations were happening in the West and were very expensive. Aravind went ahead by deciding to get into manufacturing the intraocular lens in 1992, making it more affordable, to change things in India.

Says R.D. Thulasiraj, 'We decided that we will be committed to doing a 10X disruption—that is, we will price the same tech at one-tenth of the market price, but the products will be of the same quality.' Today Aurolab employs over 1,000 people and has 10 to 12 per cent of the global market in terms of the number of lenses sold (by number of units). Alongside, Aravind also commenced a surgical training programme for doctors and professors, who would train their students in hospitals. Aravind also set up such surgical training programmes outside of its institution. Aravind alone, over the years has trained around 6,000 doctors. In Uttar Pradesh alone, about 100 government doctors have been trained.

Aravind's unique approach to scaling has been a key factor in its growth and success. The organization's approach, known as 'external scaling', differs from the typical commercial metric of scaling to improve top and bottom lines and market share. Aravind considers itself a socially driven organization and thus its primary goal is to achieve its purpose of reducing or eliminating preventable blindness. In this context, the 'top line' refers to its success in achieving its social mission rather than financial metrics.

Aravind Eye Care System's growth has been driven by its commitment to reach the unreached by continually improving its technology and innovations, both in administration and eye-care delivery. For example in 1983, R.D. Thulasiraj introduced computers brought from the US for patient registration. As mentioned, Aravind Eye Care System was also an early adopter of intraocular lenses, which were not yet widely used at the time. The lenses provided significant benefits, particularly for rural patients who worked in the fields and previously had to wear thick glasses post-surgery. The introduction of intraocular lenses allowed them to regain their sight and continue working without hindrance.

Dr R. Kim, Aravind's chief medical officer, explains that the organization's constant commitment to being at the forefront of technology has been a key factor in its success. Aravind was an early adopter of innovative technologies, such as the fax machine and data modem, which were not widely used in the region at that time. Today, they are using artificial intelligence to screen diabetic patients for diabetic retinopathy. This focus on being cutting-edge has helped Aravind thrive over the years.

Dr V envisioned Aravind as a trusteeship model in which family members act as trustees, so although Aravind appears to embrace modernity it is deeply influenced by Dr V's spirituality and philosophy that emphasizes money should not be the ultimate goal.

Evolve Back Resorts (Ramapuram Holdings): Bengaluru

The Ramapuram family traces its origins to a small town called Pala in the district of Kottayam, Kerala. The family has lived through extraordinary events such as the two World Wars and has played a prominent part in the country's freedom struggle, whilst establishing itself in business without compromising its values and patriotism.

Though Thomas E. Ramapuram is recognized as the modern-day founder of Ramapuram Holdings, it was his father Emmanuel Ramapuram, born in 1889, who laid the early foundations of the group. He was appointed as a Ranger (eyes and ears for wildlife protection) at a very young age and put in charge of South Canara and Coorg under the Madras Presidency. He learnt the lay of the land and soon fell in love with the region. However, a severe bout of malaria led to his admission to Father Muller Hospital, Mangalore. Upon recovery and return to Pala, he studied and then practiced law. As founder-president of the Pala Committee of the Indian National Congress, he also participated actively in the freedom struggle and was imprisoned several times during this period.

At the age of thirty-four Emmanuel travelled to Coorg to purchase the Chikkanahalli and Kaimakumbatta Estates from Percy Tipping, managing director (MD), Consolidated Coffee Estates Ltd, incorporated in Great Britain. Later, he went on to acquire Somangad Estate, Coorg, Karnataka, in 1938 and Somerville Estate, Kannur, Kerala, in 1941.

After Emmanuel Ramapuram's untimely demise, his eldest son, Thomas E. Ramapuram (Sunny), took over the family business at the tender age of twenty-one. A progressive person of that era, he graduated in 1941 from Madras Christian College and also pursued B.Sc. Agriculture in Coimbatore. Within four years of taking over from his father, Thomas acquired the Sampigacolly Estate in Coorg. With this acquisition the family's portfolio of plantations made it a significant private holder in Coorg; they now owned around 1,500 acres of prime plantations. Later, in 1961, he acquired Santa Maria Estate, Thrissur, Kerala. He and his two brothers further expanded their holdings, including the addition of the Santa Maria Estate in Thrissur, Kerala, and in 1961 they divided the (around) 1,800 acres of plantations among the three of them.

After the family partition, all was well until 1975, when the smoke house at the rubber plantation caught fire at the height of the production season. However, the loss did not deter Thomas. His priceless advice to his children then was: 'do not put all your eggs in one basket'. In that spirit, the family set up Kerala Rubbers in Thrissur, Kerala—one of the first centrifuged latex plants in the country. By this time, the seven sons of

Thomas E. Ramapuram were finishing their studies and starting their careers in various parts of the family business in plantations and manufacturing. Business beckoned them to Mangalore in 1975, where they set up a carton manufacturing factory.

Once a planter, always a planter. The family identified about 1,000 acres of virgin land in Kundapur near Mangalore and started planting rubber saplings. After that, land was bought near Mangalore to set up a crumb rubber factory that was eventually shelved. The latest acquisition of Ramapuram Holdings is the 2,500-acre Elkhill Group of Estates from the Bombay Burmah Trading Company (BBTC) in 2023. In 1991, Thomas' youngest son Jose Ramapuram was dispatched to Dubai, first to start a spices trading business and then a real estate marketing firm. Both had initial successes but did not sustain long enough. Undaunted, the family looked ahead.

While Thomas E. Ramapuram inculcated vision and values in his seven sons, his wife Thraciamma gilded this with spirituality. To her goes the singular credit of laying the family's spiritual foundations that would help it weather the storms of life and the changes wrought by time. Sadly, in the early 1990s, Thomas Ramapuram was detected with cancer. He lived to see his seven sons set up their first resort in 1994, as a timeshare, under the brand name of Orange County Resorts (Coorg is famous for oranges apart from coffee) at the family's 300-acre plantation in Coorg.

Thomas Ramapuram passed away in 1997 at the age of seventy-five. The virtues of 'integrity, high thinking and simple living' that he advocated throughout his life were to become the cornerstones of the Ramapuram family's philosophy and, later, its corporate ethics. Meanwhile, with business booming at

Orange County Resorts, it was converted to a full-fledged luxury resort. Success begets success and the second resort at Kabini was followed by a third at Hampi, one after another.

In 2015, the group entered the real estate business through luxury Earthitects Private Residences. In 2017, Orange County Resorts rebranded itself as Evolve Back Resorts and more recently, it established its first overseas resort in Botswana. Ramapuram Holdings has also acquired land for resorts at Paro in Bhutan, Mandu in Madhya Pradesh and Kumta in Karwar, Karnataka. The latest acquisition of Ramapuram Holdings is the 2,500-acre Elkhill Group of Estates in Sidapur, in Kodagu district in Coorg, from the Bombay Burmah Trading Company (BBTC) in 2023. With this acquisition the group has moved into the fast-moving foods business with its 'Sidapur' brand of coffee experiences.

Currently Ramapuram Holdings operates in four verticals—Plantations, Hospitality, Real Estate and FMCG. It now seems that there is no looking back. Sums up Jose Ramapuram, director, Evolve Back Resorts, 'My father was always very keen that we must experiment and not be afraid to fail. This philosophy and our faith in God have helped us overcome many challenges.'

Today, the legacy of Thomas E. Ramapuram is being taken forward by his seven sons: Emmanuel, Abe, Thomas, George, Cherian, Dr John and Jose. With five among the seven cousins—sons of the seven brothers—joining the group, the process of passing on the baton of responsibility has commenced. Groomed to take on the mantle of leadership within the group, the future of the legacy bequeathed by Thomas E. Ramapuram resides in their safe hands.

Popular Automobiles (Kuttukaran Group): Kochi

Popular Automobiles was started in 1944 in Trichur (now Thrissur, Kerala) by K.P. Paul. He was inspired by the entrepreneurial spirit of his mother who ran a small industry involved in hand-pounding rice. In those days, large volumes of rice would arrive by ship from Akyab and Rangoon to Trichur, which was a hub for industry and business at that time. There were no machines to process the rice.

Paul started his career at the age of twelve, when he began working as a clerk in Rice Bazar at Trichur. Picking up his basics in no time, he moved to a provisions store at Nayarangadi, Trichur. After working at the shop for a while, the owner started leaving the shop to Paul for long stretches, going home for lunch, and returning in the evening. Paul would be left to take care of the shop. Gradually, he picked up the nuances of business. He realized that he could run the store proficiently, that the owner had enough confidence in his abilities. Why should I be doing this for somebody else, he wondered, why not do this for myself?

'In 1936, my father was the first person in Kerala to carry a communist flag and walk in a procession,' says Popular Director John Paul. 'This was in 1936. By 1939, he had become an entrepreneur.' He was twenty-five and World War II was just about to begin. Jobs were very difficult to find. His parents were worried and upset, but he decided to stand by his decision to not work for anybody else.

His firm stance probably convinced his mother who pitched in with some capital when he decided to begin with a washing home (laundry). In less than a year, his business, Popular Washing Home, was flourishing. 'There was a reason why it was called a "washing home" and not a laundry,' explains John Paul. 'The name was meant to assure customers that the quality of the laundry service would match that of their home. He always had that customer-oriented outlook.'

However, K.P. Paul's heart was not in the laundry business. He had always been fascinated by automobiles and had a craving for doing something in the automobile industry. He could not venture into it in the beginning as he did not have the capital. He started small, with cycle, battery and tyre repairs. The repair shop carried on the business name, it was called Popular Industrials.

Within a month, he realized that focusing on the tyre business would bring in the money. 'These were not new tyres he was dealing in, but second-hand tyres. Because by 1940, there was a shortage of virtually everything,' says John Paul. 'The tyres he was servicing were basically for trucks and buses—there were hardly any cars. Cars became a good business much later.'

People would come in, get their tyres repaired and wait for hours together for the tyres to be re-vulcanized. This gave him the idea to keep some repaired tyres ready. 'He thought he could give it to them and probably they could save their valuable time,' says John Paul.

Now K.P. Paul started selling refurbished second-hand tyres. He would go to Coimbatore, find some used tyres, repair them and keep them in his shop. The repair shop became a second-hand tyre business. He started getting repeat customers who would ask for particular pieces, or place orders for other specific automobile parts. This is how he gradually ventured into the automobile business. Later on, he would also get goods that he knew would move faster.

With the end of World War II in 1945, a large number of automobile spares came in from military disposals in Burma and other places. There were many American vehicles that were running for the British army at that time; these vehicles were coming back and the spares were getting sold as military disposals.

The first branch of Popular Automobiles—though it was for sourcing—was opened after Partition. It was, however, not opened anywhere in Kerala, but in Calcutta (now Kolkata) in West Bengal. This happened because of K.P. Paul's diligence and persistence in sourcing the best spare parts. He found that when he went to Bangalore (now Bengaluru) to source something, he would be told that the parts were coming from Calcutta!

Then he learnt that spares were coming in from Shillong—the military was auctioning spares there. But with the Partition, the journey from Shillong to Calcutta by truck had become much longer. What used to take a week would now take a month or more. So he would make a list of the spares and send it across to all the known bus houses in South India. 'We had customers from all over the region. He always placed emphasis on the reliability of the source. His motto was—if you come to our shop, you will always get what you are looking for,' says John Paul.

Popular Automobiles and the Kuttukaran Group have come a long way in the last eight decades, as we will see in later chapters.

Today, the company employs over 9,000 people and has a turnover of about Rs 5,000 crore.

ELICO Ltd: Hyderabad

Founded by the current chairman, Ramesh Datla's uncle, DVS Raju, in 1960, who moved back from the United Kingdom to India, ELICO is the first analytical instrumentation company in India that laid the foundation for the analytical instrumentation industry in the country. Growing slowly and laboriously by developing indigenous technologies sometimes in collaboration with government research institutions, the Indian market was definitely not easy to crack.

When it started, ELICO was operating under the pre-liberalization regime. Until the 1990s, private industry was not a big buyer in India; the market was dominated by government procurement. Industry became a big buyer only after liberalization, when government rules and restrictions on local trades and businesses were eased. Technology and instrumentation were mostly budgetary purchases before liberalization. Companies like ELICO have had an evolutionary process of growth.

Apart from market challenges, ELICO also had its share of family struggles in the growth journey. Key among them was succession. Even after it was decided that Ramesh would take over from his uncle as the chairman, his uncle, being from the earlier generation and the founder to boot, wanted to have his way of doing things. But that was not the preferred route for Ramesh as he just got back from working in the USA and had a very different approach on innovation and running the company.

Eventually, Ramesh bought over the controlling share from all his family members and began charting out a new course for the company to become a global player.

The Indian instrumentation market was quite fragile and fragmented and totally dominated by multinational companies. ELICO was founded in 1960, and another four companies came up, but three of them did not last long. One that did was the public sector Electronic Corporation of India Ltd (ECIL). Today, most of ELICO's competition is from small companies in north India, especially around Ambala in Punjab. However, Ramesh Notes that 'most of them are traders who bring products from China and put Indian labels on them. I feel the AatmaNirbhar Bharat campaign has spoilt the whole market because people put the "Made in India" logo and start selling.'

Moreover, the global instrumentation market is dominated by the West: about 70 per cent of the market is controlled by American companies. The technologies also originate in the US. Of the top ten companies, around seven to eight are American, and the remainder are from Japan and Europe. Outside the West, it is only China that is slowly trying to come up in this area and has successfully captured the lower end of the market. India is caught in this market cauldron.

ELICO's journey has been punctuated not only by such market challenges but also by policy challenges. For example, in the late 1990s, instrumentation products were classified as IT products by the government as per the WTO agreement, which brought down import duties from 110 per cent to zero by 2005. The ensuing duty regime change was an impetus for the company to move up the value chain to higher value-added products.

What impeded ELICO's growth was the lack of a strong knowledge base in India. Very few universities taught instrumentation or had instrumentation departments that conducted research. The domain is considered unattractive as not many students are interested in studying such complexities where product research and development takes quite a number of years. Analytical instrumentation involves multidisciplinary sciences and engineering, as one would have to study physics, chemistry, software, hardware (digital, analog), mechanics and optics, among others.

The company also addressed the lack of a strong knowledge base in India.

To develop a good instrumentation product was taking around four years. About 15 years back, ELICO took up the initiative to collaborate with universities to develop knowledge and skills in the analytical instrumentation domain. Developing collaborations with universities in tier-two towns like Krishnadevaraya University in Anantpur were focused, which had an instrumentation department and an M.Sc. course in instrumentation. 'We would give our own problems for their project work and the project would be done in our R&D department. That is how we started developing technologies. Later, we started doing joint PhD programmes as well, where the research scholar was on our employee rolls and worked on our focus areas. We gave them our problems and they worked their thesis on arriving at solutions while creating IP and patents,' says Ramesh Datla. The model became quite successful and ELICO roped in the Confederation of Indian Industry (CII) to adopt it. Around 2008, CII proposed this model to the Ministry of Science and Technology. In 2010, the Indian government announced the launch of the PM Fellowship programmes for joint research with industry. Says Ramesh, 'Today, we work with three universities—NIT Warangal, Raichur University and Anantpur University. Our model is that we give the problem and the funding. We think of ourselves more as techno-preneurs than commercial-minded people. We are happier when we develop a new technology, not so much when it is translated into business.' Not quite sure though if Vanitha Datla would agree!

'One disagreement that I always had with my husband, Ramesh, was that we were not adequately focused on the commercial aspects of the business', confesses Vanitha. 'Finance is my domain and I always look at the financial and commercial aspects of the business, because that is what will help us sustain in the long run'. 'When I got married to Ramesh in 1986, the corporate world was not very welcoming to women, and in family firms, women family members were very rarely given a chance to enter the business.' But Vanitha was not one to sit at home and be content with domestic duties as she had dreams of becoming a surgeon like her father. 'Destiny seems to have had other plans for me,' says Vanitha as she approached her maternal grandfather for a job in his companies. Being in the hard core building materials manufacturing sector such as cement, refractories, ceramics, etc., he couldn't find her a position in those fields, as they were reserved for the male scions of the family, but rather placed her in the group's financial services company.

Vanitha had to struggle for her share of responsibilities and rights primarily because she was never groomed for the work place nor was she qualified at that point in time. She took up the challenge to get herself a couple of Master's degrees and certificates and learnt on the job, how to navigate her career. She credits Ramesh for introducing the world of networking to her and she began to get very active in the industry forums such as Confederation of Indian Industry (CII). 'I feel that I had to prove my mettle in the outside world to be taken seriously in my own company. To be quite frank, I was playing second fiddle in the business for quite a while but today, we are co-preneurs,' says Vanitha. Ramesh appreciates her role now. It is not often that Indian family businesses are managed successfully by husband–wife duos. Hyderabad-based ELICO Ltd is an exception.

Sandu Pharmaceuticals: Mumbai

'After the discovery of penicillin in the late 1800s, the British taxed Indian medicines to capture the world market,' notes Shashank Sandu, non-executive director, Sandu Pharmaceuticals Ltd. 'It was at this time that Lokmanya Tilak delivered his historic declaration for Swaraj (self-rule) and swadeshi. Tilak had met my grandfather and advised him to set up a practice in a place that needed his skills.'

That is how Shashank's grandfather (and his four brothers), who had an ayurvedic practice in Rajapur in Ratnagiri district, Maharashtra, decided to move to Mumbai to set up a clinic in Thakurdwar in Kalbadevi, where they gave medical advice. The other brothers stayed back in Konkan to look after their land. In Mumbai, the brothers encountered several challenges when it came to sourcing quality raw materials. To solve this problem, they decided to do a backward integration with the medicines via admixtures or formulations. And this is how the Sandu brothers set up a rudimentary formulation company in Thakurdwar.

The practice began in a two-room clinic and soon expanded to three dispensaries, each run by one of the three brothers. 'My father and uncle were among the first qualified Ayurvedacharyas,' says Shashank. 'In those days, "naadi pariksha", or reading the pulse, was important, and they were well trained in that. Because of their skill in diagnosing ailments and prescribing the right medicine, they became quite popular.' Another key reason for their success was that they were never motivated by profit in what they did. Service to society was always the goal. It was often the case that they would charge patients a nominal sum or treat them for free, depending on their economic situation.

Kalbadevi was known as the 'davaa' or medicine bazaar of the country at that time, as this was where most of the medicines were imported to and distributed. And the Sandu family's clinics flourished here. Their practice grew as they started doing things in a more organized manner. The requirement for medication went up drastically and more people joined the team, including women, who would be mostly involved in cleaning operations, segregation, and sorting, at this stage. The compounding part would be done by the Ayurvedacharyas themselves, as that was the established process.

The Sandu brothers used typical kilns to make the 'rasa-aushadi' via the titration method. Heat over 270 degrees celsius was generated through these kilns and medicines were formulated using extraction and filtration processes (the latter done using a fine cotton cloth). The fermentation chambers in these drums—where the asavarishtas or the kashayam were stored—are very similar to a winery or a brewery. They were monitored and numbered, with a number assigned to each product. The in-process testing was very organized and modern, though the methods they were following are mentioned in the scriptures or the Vedas.

When demand grew, they had to shift from the 'davaa' bazaar of Kalbadevi to a place where they could set up a manufacturing unit. They chose Chembur, an area cut off from the mainland or main city. Chembur was chosen to ensure that the manufacturing process was well laid out, and perfectly organized. New recruits had to be brought in as demand for manpower spiked when the operations grew. Women were also brought in as staff as the demand grew, and they would work mostly in the packaging processes. Sandu employed people who were from the villages of Konkan Rajapur. They were resettled in Chembur, given residential accommodation, and their families were also rehabilitated and given work. 'This was a very unusual thing in those days,' points out Shashank. 'It was hard to find women working at that time, he says, that too in a factory operation.'

Today, Sandu is a name established throughout India and has earned acceptance even beyond its borders and, that too, not just with the Indian diaspora. For over 125 years, the secret of Sandu's success lies in its commitment to quality and firm adherence to the basic tenets of Ayurveda. Today, the fourth-generation scion of the Sandu family at the helm implements a seamless confluence between tradition and modern pharmaceutical practices, such as the use of high-pressure, sophisticated, and expensive equipment, costing around Rs 50 lakh each.

Today, much of Chembur reflects the story of Sandu Pharma. 'You can see that in our address—Sandu Pharmaceuticals Ltd, Sandu Nagar, DK Sandu Marg, Chembur, Mumbai 71. In those days, this entire area was known as Sandu Nagar.'

Fast forward 125 years from its nationalistic beginnings and its commitment to quality is reflected in the ISO 9001:2000 certification it has earned for its group operations, which include manufacturing units at New Mumbai and Goa, as well as the full-fledged research unit, Sandu Research Foundation Pvt Ltd, in Goa.

Gera Developments: Pune

The Gera family's roots are in pre-Partition India, in Quetta, now in Pakistan. Kumar Gera, the youngest of two siblings, was born in Quetta. His father, Pritamdas Gera was involved in the mining business in Baluchistan, Karachi and Quetta. Kumar Gera was just a year old when the family (parents and an elder brother who now lives in Goa) moved to Pune in 1947 as refugees. They chose Pune because a friend of their father's lived in the city. He assisted the Geras in the initial months till they were able to find their feet.

Things stabilized a bit in the early 1950s when his father was able to get some monetary claims from the government: enough to restart their life and also start a business. Pritamdas Gera chose the field of contracting, doing government contracts that required less capital and some knowledge about construction. Kumar Gera and his brother studied at an engineering college in Pune, graduated as civil engineers, and joined their father's business, many years later in the 1960s.

In the early 1970s, their business suffered due to a hike in oil prices. At that time, they were working on building projects in Pune and Goa. Since they had fixed-rate contracts with the government, there was no escalation. In Goa, they were hammered so badly that they almost went bust. Kumar Gera's brother decided to exit the family business and settled in Goa. Kumar and his father finished off whatever contracts were left and moved into real estate development.

With little interest in contracting, Kumar Gera wanted to be an architect. His father had a plot that he had been given in exchange for some of his properties in Pakistan. They started their first real-estate venture there in December 1972 by building ten bungalows. The business took off and saw a continuous, steady growth.

'I was very fortunate that my-father-in-law was in the same business in Pune,' says Kumar Gera. 'He was actually the pioneer of ownership apartments in Pune and Mumbai. He was a very ethical person, and highly respected. So, on one side, I had him to learn from, and on the other, I had my father who could teach me about the contracting part. I had the advantage of being able to assimilate knowledge from both,' he says. His wife, Nalini, has been a pillar of support to him in business and family.

He learnt several things on the entrepreneurial and business side from his family. He credits his father-in-law for teaching him the benefits of ethics as a builder and developer (as builders and developers were 'not highly regarded by the general public'). He recounts a time when his father-in-law was selling flats for about Rs 20,000 each. 'This was in the early days when the concept of ownership apartments was introduced. The initial deposit for the flats would be about Rs 2,000. Very often, people would just leave the amount with him in cash, coming back to make the agreement later. Sometimes people would change their mind and want the amount back. He would give it back without batting an eyelid and not harp on about commitments. Then there were cases when, due to inflation, prices would go up. But he would stick to his commitment to buyers even when he was not making any money on the project. In those days, escalation clauses were not built into agreements. Even now they are not; you are expected to take care of it on your own.'

On the construction side, Gera learnt about the value of frugality from his father. He learned that it is important to look after, and look at, every rupee. Which is perhaps why Gera was always keen to build a good image for his company. And he also tried to improve the image of the industry through associations like the Confederation of Real Estate Developers Association of India (CREDAI). Till the late 1990s, it was known as the Promoters and Builders Association.

It has been about fifty years since Gera Developments started. There have been lean years, some bad years, and lots of ups and downs, for instance, in 1976, when Indira Gandhi introduced the Urban Land Ceiling Act which crippled growth. This Act was scrapped in the late 1990s, and Gera incidentally, had a significant part to play in terms of lobbying and influencing the government. 'It so happened that the minister concerned was very close to our family. The ministry was under Ram Jethmalani at that time. We met him in Pune, at his house which is next door to mine (which he had bought from my father-in-law; he also bought his next house from me). We were able to convince him to repeal the Act, which he ultimately had done.'

Sixty-two projects and approximately 6 million square feet of development later, Gera Developments has won the trust of 8,000+ customers. Within India, the group has projects in Pune, Goa and Bengaluru. It has also started four real estate development projects in USA. Today, Gera Developments is global.

Dodla Dairy: Hyderabad

When twenty-three-year-old industrial engineer Sunil Dodla Reddy decided to become an entrepreneur, he chose an unrelated field—exporting Indian mangoes to Singapore. His consignment was rejected when it did not meet the stringent standards. Undeterred, this native of Nellore district in Andhra Pradesh reached out to friends in Singapore, who got down to sorting and grading the mangoes in one of their apartments. Reddy managed to sell most of the (now graded) mangoes that he had exported, in the local market. This minor setback did not shake his faith in doing business. But the mango-export venture did not last long, nor did two others—growing mushrooms, and trying his luck in the garment space. Dodla Dairy was his fourth attempt, and he is grateful that it has grown to where it is today.

In 1995, Reddy decided to get into the dairy business and Dodla Dairy Ltd was incorporated. The first and parent dairy plant started production in 1997 in Nellore, Andhra Pradesh. By April 1998, the corporate head office of Dodla Dairy was registered in Hyderabad. In Telangana, Dodla Dairy was processing 75,000 litres of milk a day. Reddy had raised Rs 9 crore for this purpose—Rs 5 crore as a loan from IDBI Bank and the remaining from his father Dodla Sesha Reddy. Dodla Dairy has since succeeded by consistently walking the risk-versus-growth tightrope.

Sunil Reddy cites his first acquisition, a plant in Penumuru in Chittoor district, in Andhra Pradesh, as an example. 'After we started the main Dodla Dairy, which took around Rs 7 to 8 crore as capital, we acquired another dairy in Chittoor for around Rs 40 lakh. That was in the second or third year of our operation, around 1999–2000. At that time, it was a difficult situation because of the Rs 7.5 crore, we were just about breaking even in terms of, not the profitability and EBITA [earnings before interest, taxes and amortization] of course, but the cash flows. Because we had borrowed at a 24 per cent rate of interest in those days. That was from IDBI. As an institution, they had high lending rates, and the loan was structured in a manner that you had to repay the borrowed money in five years.'

An asset acquisition of Rs 40 lakh at that stage was difficult for them, but they made a call and went ahead. 'The asset that comes into play turns us around because that Rs 40 lakh asset would give us a return of a crore to crore-and-half rupees, which then helps out the whole company. If we needed to scale up at that point of time, when there was no money, how do you raise the money? What I meant by not over-leveraging was that we were not trying to raise more debt by saying: I will somehow manage the debt,' says Reddy.

That is how Dodla Dairy operated during the initial twenty years, with a deeply embedded culture of discipline and caution whenever they were growing. 'Now we are on a cash surplus, and we still have money,' says Reddy. But he continues to err on the side of caution rather than be aggressive and scale-up unnecessarily. In 2019, the company acquired the Dindigul (Tamil Nadu)-based KC Dairy and has been able to turn around the (roughly) Rs 100 crore acquisition, and it is doing well.

Another factor that has contributed to Dodla Dairy's success is that it has been very balanced with its own greenfield projects, explains Reddy. 'The tightrope in make or buy is always a challenge. For example, we built our own greenfield recently in Hyderabad at another cost of Rs 100 crore. You have to have the confidence, get everybody together, and have people believing it and coming forward to take it. That has been our thing, saying either we can do it on our own, or can we do it by acquiring.' Also, he has preferred to not diversify, 'We did acquire one unit in Africa, for scaling. As of now, we are only doing what we know as a business.'

Expanding on the theme of discipline, Reddy says he prefers to 'not look at it as a multiple of my top line or bottom line. I look at it from a pure cash-flow point of view. If you are investing X amount of money, when are we going to get back that money, and with what kind of return?'

The company continues to aspire to do better, become bigger. 'Obviously, as we are growing, we are beginning to see the benefits of scale of operations. It's true that with that comes some associated problems. But once we move up, it also has benefits which make us stronger. That is why the scaling-up has also helped us. People need growth, everything has to keep going.'

From a turnover of about Rs 14 crore at the end of its first year of operations, Dodla Dairy has milked a business of about Rs 2,800 crores (as of 23 March 2023). Not a bad deal for a three-time failed serial entrepreneur!

Bhima Jewellers: Kochi

A person familiar with South India would conjure up visions of tasty dosas and Udupi restaurants, when hearing of Udupi. Therefore, it is perhaps not surprising that when Udupi-born (1904) K. Lakshminarayana Bhattar, popularly known as Bhima Bhattar, moved to the peaceful town of Alleppey in Kerala, he chose to live with his brother-in-law and help out at his restaurant, Girija Nivas, after school hours. However, he had to discontinue his further education at college due to financial difficulties. Saddened, he resolved to become financially independent and started a small business, selling perfumes and cosmetics at Girija Nivas while still working there.

After his marriage to Vanaja, the young couple settled in Alleppey where Bhima Bhattar realized that the profit from his fledgling business was insufficient for a comfortable married life. One of his acquaintances mentioned to him that the demographic situation in Alleppey was congenial for a profitable business in silver jewellery, cutlery, and puja articles. It was when Bhima was mulling over this that a customer at the restaurant asked him whether Bhima could supply him with two silver tumblers. Now the only concern was how to procure the silver. Vanaja had a pair of heavy silver anklets that she gladly gave her husband when he told her of his quandary.

Using these, Bhima had the tumblers made, and displayed these at the restaurant. Soon, demand for Bhima's silver articles grew in leaps and bounds. It was at this stage that Bhima Bhattar met Madhavan Pillai and the duo started a business in gold jewellery called Alleppey Emporium. They parted ways a year later and Bhima started off on his own, dealing in gold and silver jewellery. Thus was laid the foundation of Bhima's golden empire.

Bhima's honest practices ensured the rapid growth of his business. During World War II, when trade in gold jewellery of lower quality was rampant, Bhima's 22 carat jewellery was the beacon of trust. With hard work and innovative practices, Bhima Jewellers of Mullakkal, Alleppey attained a legendary status, soon becoming the hub for gold wholesale trade in Kerala. The wholesale business was done in the showroom premises after 10 p.m., and catered to the demand of retailers all over Kerala. Bhima Bhattar is also responsible to a large extent for the paradigm shift in Kerala's jewellery trade from made-to-order jewellery to today's readymade jewellery. The Bhima showroom in Alleppey that exists even today, was undoubtedly the first showroom of readymade gold jewellery in Kerala.

He was also one of the first diamond merchants in the state and introduced Navaratna jewellery. Bhima Bhattar changed the perception of a retail jewellery showroom with changes that were unheard of at that time. His showroom was tastefully done;

never had the people of the region seen a jewellery showroom of such splendour. His was also perhaps the first air-conditioned jewellery showroom in Kerala.

The Gold Control Act enacted by Parliament in 1962 after the Indo-China war brought with it a slump in trade. As soon as some leniency came about in the Gold Control Act in 1968, Bhima Bhattar, now assisted by his five sons, consolidated his position as the foremost jeweller in Kerala. In 1978, he opened a showroom in M.G. Road, Ernakulam (Kochi), which became the most renowned jewellery retail store in the state. The demise of Vanaja on 22 June 1984 came as a shock to Bhima Bhattar. He believed that she was the source of his success and good fortune.

After the abolition of the Gold Control Act in 1992, the Bhima brand gradually spread its presence within Kerala and also in Tamil Nadu and Karnataka. Today, the Bhima Group, with the cheerful Bhima Boy as its trademark, is administered by the five sons of Bhima Bhattar. Though the showrooms are managed separately, it is the set of values infused by its illustrious founder that is the backbone of the entire group. Relations with the public are maintained as a unified brand that gratefully acknowledges and enjoys an unparalleled trust since 1925—Bhima Gold, Pure Gold.

The flagship Bhima Jewels store is located in Kochi and managed by Bhima Bhattar's son, B. Bindumadhav. Bindumadhav joined the jewellery industry as a teenager with his first position in sales. He was a quick learner and has played a key role in introducing many new ideas and concepts to the market. Under Bindumadhav's guidance and game-changing vision of how jewellery should be procured and sold in the retail market, Bhima has expanded its operations and product portfolio to better serve customers. Bindumadhav's son, Abhishek, represents the third generation of the family and has been involved in all aspects of the company. He has been instrumental in launching Bhima Boutique and is executing his father's and grandfather's vision, taking the organization to the next level with a fashion-forward outlook.

House of Anita Dongre: Mumbai

Anita Dongre was raised in Mumbai along with five siblings and they spent their summer holidays in Jaipur. The family was very close and in 1995, Anita, along with her brother Mukesh Sawlani and sister Meena Sehra, founded AND Designs India (now renamed House of Anita Dongre).

Realizing that there was a lack of quality women's western wear brands in India, in 1997 AND Designs India launched a western-wear brand 'AND'. This was a significant milestone for Anita Dongre. Through informal market surveys, she discovered that people were purchasing imported clothing from China and Thailand because there were no Indian brands that catered to the specific fits and sizes of Indian women. This was addressed too.

When the brand 'AND' was started, there was a misconception that it was tailored around her name An and D: Anita Dongre. A lot of people thought that. It was not so. The brand 'AND' was just coined; it did not have any resonance to her name. But a lot of people still think that 'AND' is derived from Anita Dongre.

The decade following the launch of the AND brand saw smooth progression and growth for the business, with no major obstacles. Their own retail stores played a significant role in this growth, with the first store being opened in Mumbai's Crossroads Mall. In 2007, Anita Dongre and her siblings launched the brand 'Global Desi', after recognizing that while the western wear market was significant, the ethnic wear segment was ten times larger. By 2010, they had realized the importance of sustainable fashion and in 2012 they launched the 'Grassroot' brand. This was partly an initiative to support and promote Indian artisans. It was an early effort towards sustainability in the fashion industry.

Anita Dongre has been a trailblazer in the fashion industry by creating avenues for Indian artisans to market their products. Through the Anita Dongre Foundation, she has provided countless rural women with livelihood opportunities and skill training, giving them a voice in society. As an ethical vegan, environmentalist, and advocate for compassionate living, she refuses to use any fur or leather in her designs. For Anita, the Grassroot brand represents her core passions—designing beautiful clothes with a purpose, while sustaining ancient Indian crafts and promoting sustainability. She believes in doing good for both artisans and the planet, especially women artisans in villages who are the custodians of these crafts.

In 2007, the House of Anita Dongre also received private equity investment from Future Group, marking another significant milestone. Six years later, in 2013, Future Group exited and global PE firm General Atlantic came in, bringing about significant changes. The company began to professionalize itself, implementing systems and processes, and introducing governance systems to ensure the institution's longevity beyond the founders.

During the investment by General Atlantic, there was a focus on ensuring the brand's sustainability even after Anita Dongre's involvement, a challenge that many fashion brands face. The introduction of strong governance institutions within the group followed the classical process of well-managed family groups. Prior to General Atlantic's investment, the group's revenue averaged around Rs 150 crore, but today it is believed to have crossed over Rs 800 crore in less than a decade, a clear demonstration of the power of scale.

Says Mukesh Sawlani, 'A number of global investors were chasing us to invest in the company but we decided to go with General Atlantic because they had a global perspective. We knew that sooner than later we would go global. And they are a great fund to work with. Their value systems match ours. It was a wise decision.'

House of Anita Dongre quietly built their empire, which currently extends to five brands: AND, her western wear brand for women, with 125 stores; Global Desi, her boho-chic line, with 138 outlets; Grassroot, her youngest brand that focuses on sustainable luxury, with four stores; her couture line Anita Dongre, with twelve stand-alone outlets, and a flagship store each in New York and Dubai.

Adds Mukesh Sawlani, 'In our generation there are six of us. I would give credit to our parents and our upbringing for the sustainability of our family institution. Because we are very close as a family, we don't have egos. We have all shed our egos years ago. So, in that dynamic, it does not matter if Anita got all the limelight. And, also as people, Meena and I are more introverts and we do not like the limelight, especially me. We are very, very comfortable if Anita takes all the limelight. And of course, it is also a lot of hard work for her as the Creative Head and the face of the institution globally.'

With the next generation of the family joining the business and global iconic customers who would be the envy of any business group, the House of Anita Dongre is a perfect balance of all that matters when building a scalable, long-lasting family business.

IBS Software (Offices Worldwide)

Kizhakkambalam is a small village on the outskirts of the city of Kochi. More than forty years back, it was unknown even within the state of Kerala. But today, it has gained prominence because of the nearby presence of two large companies, Synthite and Kitex and the village boy, Valayil Korath (V.K.) Mathews, the founder of IBS Software.

Mathews did his M.Tech. from IIT Kanpur in aeronautical engineering; IIT Kanpur and the Indian Institute of Science (IISc) Bengaluru being the first two institutions to offer aeronautical engineering programmes in the country. His research work for the thesis had complex differential equations to solve using numerical methods and algorithms, which required extensive use of computers. Thus, he ended up using the computers, computer programming and numerical methods a lot. This exposure went on to have a defining impact on his career later in life. Mind you, this was in 1978, when computers had not percolated down to the common man in India. It was much later in the mid-1980s when then prime minister, Rajiv Gandhi, ushered in the early computer era in the country.

Thereafter, Mathews joined the Military College of Electrical and Mechanical Engineering at Hyderabad, where he had all the privileges of an army officer without the rigours of military life. After that, he joined Air India in the IT Department in Mumbai (then Bombay) when it was computerizing its reservation processes around the world. Airlines were one of the early adopters of computer technology because of the need for synchronized information across geographies. After two years in the commercial capital of India, he joined Emirates in Dubai in 1983, again in the IT Department. He stayed with the airline for about fourteen years, moving up the ladder steadily becoming the general manager and head of IT systems. By this time, he was an accomplished technology specialist and the pangs of entrepreneurship began.

In October 1997, he finally quit Emirates and shifted to Thiruvananthapuram (then Trivandrum) the capital of Kerala, to start IBS Software. Incidentally, the company was inaugurated by then chief minister, E.K. Nayanar, and Susheela Gopalan, the industry minister, both of whom were from the ruling Left government that was not in favour of computerization. During those days IBM (International Business Machines) was the reigning global computer company. Mathews drew inspiration from IBM and called his company IBS Software. The rest, as they say, is history.

Expert Take by M.S.A. Kumar

- The above case studies of twelve family businesses have a few common threads running through them. Transformation and growth of family businesses is a long journey of ups and downs and the ultimate goal can be achieved only through endurance and patience. Carrying the family members along in a harmonious set-up through right communication holds the key.
- In accomplishing any goal, the company of like-minded people by your side makes it all the better. Wise counsel comes from them when you face a difficulty or a crisis.
- Aspirations are possibilities, so the family entrepreneurs quoted in this book have kept them high. Aspirational vision and goals, even while sounding like dreams and utopia, release the team's energies. Dr Venkataswami's (Aravind Eye Hospital) vision 'to eliminate needless blindness' is a case in point. One key learning which comes across well is, 'Push the boundaries of what you thought is possible and don't be afraid of failure.'

In all the twelve cases, they all believed in one thing: no matter what you achieve, your best is yet to come. Transformation of a family business is not about making a caterpillar crawl faster, but making it into a beautiful butterfly. And it is this battle between mind and mindset that is necessary for transformation.

3

MINDSET FOR THE LONG HAUL

Think Big, Stay Focused and Take Balanced Risks

TO OVERCOME THE CHALLENGES OF GROWTH AND longevity there are a number of routes that family business entrepreneurs and companies can take. Some of these include governance, succession planning, going global, professionalization and building a great brand. But all of these are later steps and will be incomplete unless there is a fundamental starting point: mindset for growth. This mindset can be inbuilt in an entrepreneur's psyche or it can be a part of the family business's DNA. There are also ways to acquire it through formal learning in business schools or through corporate training. Exposures through networking can influence the mindset positively. There are also many facets to this growth mindset.

However, we will discuss three aspects—think big; stay focused; take balanced risks—through three (Eastern Condiments, IBS Software and Dodla Dairy) of the twelve case studies. These three family businesses have gone on to acquire a national and global scale of operations and size that would help them move from generation to generation.

Eastern Condiments: Thinking Big

When the Norwegian food giant Orkla ASA inked an agreement for a majority stake in Eastern Condiments in 2020, it was the high point of a journey that started three-and-a-half decades ago in a remote village in Kerala. Although Eastern Condiments started in a small way, as Eastern Coffee and Curry Powder in Adimali, it has been able to come so far and scale-up because of the mindset of its promoters—think big.

Two critical dimensions have defined thinking big at Eastern: (i) flexibility of thinking demonstrated by M.E. Meeran even though he was a traditional first-generation entrepreneur; (ii) the ability of his sons, Navas and Firoz, to dream of an organization that would partner with some of the best companies in India and overseas, such as United States (US)-based McCormick & Co, and later with Norway's Orkla ASA and its Indian subsidiary MTR Foods. These partnerships have helped the company scale, grow from Rs 380 crore in FY 2010 to Rs 1,085 crore in FY 2023, and unlock value. As of 2023, Eastern Condiments exports to the Gulf Cooperation Council (GCC) countries, the US, the UK, Canada, Europe, Singapore, Malaysia, Maldives, Yemen, and Australia, among others.

Eastern Condiments, as it exists now, was born as an afterthought when the founder, M.E. Meeran, decided to do something different from his provision store and distributorship business in 1983. Coffee was his first choice; he ground coffee beans into powder and sold it. But the businessman in him was not satisfied with one product. He liked to think big and perhaps it is this trait that has helped the company immensely in its onward progress. 'Why not try to sell chilli, turmeric and coriander powder along with the coffee,' he thought. A bank loan helped in expanding space to accommodate additional grinding machines in Adimali.

In the event, coffee took a backseat and sales of spice products surged. Realizing that spices would be the mainstay of the company in future, Meeran devoted more time, adding more products as time went by. In the 1980s the domestic spice industry was in its infancy, with just a handful of firms in India. With nuclear families and working couples becoming the norm, the 1980s were the transitional phase when people were shifting to convenience foods—moving from consuming spices ground at home to buying them readymade from shops. This stood the budding company in good stead. Though the company has long since shed coffee from its name, it is still a part of the product list.

While Meeran senior laid the foundations of the company, it was his sons Navas and Firoz who ensured its evolution into a modern enterprise. Navas joined the organization in 1991, becoming CEO in 2011, and Firoz, who is fifteen years younger, joined it in 2008, becoming MD in 2014. After their entry, the company shed its traditional garb, embraced multinationals and admitted professionals from outside the family into the organization. A global vision was part of thinking big.

Perhaps the company was primed for its later tie-up with McCormick in 2010 thanks to its first brush with a multinational firm through its tie-up with the US-based private equity firm, New Vernon, in 2006. This set the tone for the future alliances. Incidentally, this was perhaps the first time that a food company from Kerala had gone in for a private equity investment. Navas took the initiative for these developments after he joined his father in steering the company.

New Vernon pumped Rs 42 crore to help fund the expansion drive of the company for five to six years and its exit in 2010 coincided with the strengthening of Eastern's determination to get a strategic partner to meet competition head-on.

The US-based McCormick & Co partnered with Eastern in 2010 and provided the company with a much-needed adrenaline push. From being just a holder of 26 per cent stake, McCormick became the guiding force making Eastern a more efficient company in all aspects. Coming as it did at a time when the spice industry in the country was galloping with many spice brands entering the fray, the tie-up proved to be a definite confidence booster.

Since there was a lot of interest in the spices sector in India, and because of other commitments that McCormick had, a new strategic partner came on board into Eastern who bought out the McCormick share, as well part of the share of the Meeran family.

McCormick would have raised its stake from 26 per cent had it not gone for a major global transaction. That perhaps may have made it think twice on increasing the stake in Eastern. So, after eight years, McCormick, while retaining its 26 per cent share, decided to end its innings as strategic partner at Eastern, satisfied that the company thrived in not just the domestic market but in many other countries in Asia, in the Middle East, US and Europe as well.

Consistent growth, an efficient workforce, a good value system, robust future prospects, strong visibility and brand recall enabled Eastern to obtain a higher valuation for the merger with Orkla. The deal implemented through Orkla's Indian subsidiary MTR Foods in 2020, valued Eastern at Rs 2,000 crore, an enviable accomplishment hitherto unheard of in the corporate history of Kerala.

The mindset of thinking big was perhaps the first step in overcoming the scaling challenge to bring Eastern Condiments to where it is now.

IBS Software: Staying Focused

IBS Software started operations in October 1997 and is today one of the largest vertical SaaS companies from India, for the world. It started with fifty-five employees from a single location in Kerala's capital city, Trivandrum (now Thiruvananthapuram), today it has over 4,000 employees from forty nationalities and operations in over forty countries.

V.K. Mathews says it is relatively more difficult to succeed in software product business because it requires significant R&D investments, domain competence and global sales and marketing. While India has access to technology talent, it falls short on domain sophistication, which is needed for building software products. This is the reason why India has many successful IT services companies, but very few enterprise software companies. The main reason that IBS succeeded where others failed was its single-minded focus on one vertical, the travel and transportation sector (aviation, hospitality, cruise).

Says Mathews, 'We have only so much energy and no more. And we were sector-focused, technology-focused and product-focused. We had huge temptations to have a diversified portfolio but we resisted them.'

The company began operations shortly before 2000 when the Y2K millennium bug, prophesied to cause havoc in computer programming, which led to the use of (legacy) software like COBALT and FORTRAN coding changes on a worldwide scale. There were huge opportunities for IBS to get on to the bandwagon and achieve scale. But Mathews let go of them and focused on developing software products for the travel and tourism industry. There were also business possibilities in body shopping, something that was rampant then. This was also given a go-by. Says Mathews, 'If I had gone in that direction, I would have been somebody else. We wouldn't have been a product company. We wouldn't have been able to get where we have reached today.'

The focus mindset was coupled with two other dimensions: purpose and strategy. These three together were a potent combination. The primary reason why IBS was founded by Mathews was not to create wealth, though that was a by-product, but to solve a critical problem to help the global airline industry function better with technology. So, all of what has been done in the last twenty-five years can be traced back to the purpose. The purpose was important, and the purpose became the focus and with this came the question of how the purpose could be achieved. The answer was simple: by helping customers achieve their business goals, all the time.

So, even though IBS is a technology company, it helps its customers achieve their business goals by helping them increase their revenue and market share, reduce their cost of operations and improve the customer experience by creating a differential construct experience. Despite being a deep technology company, its core purpose and focus are to redefine businesses in the travel and tourism industry. In the industry, the systems, technologies and the platform will always change. But what will not change is the pressure customers face to stay ahead of competition. And in that process, IBS helps them innovate, re-engineer and support those innovative processes through next-generation technologies.

Its business strategy was presented to the 2009–11 batch of the Harvard Business School's Owner President Management (OPM) programme, and it was adjudged as the best strategy in the class of 160. The OPM programme is conducted as a three-year, three-module programme with each module having twenty-one days of on-campus education. It is a highly sought-after programme among faculty members because the participants are global CEOs. Mathews' networking-mindset paid rich dividends in growing IBS. We have elaborated this aspect—leveraging the external environment through the power of networking—later in Chapter 8.

Travel and tourism has traditionally been one of the largest sectors of global GDP. In 2019, it accounted for 10.4 per cent of global GDP (USD 9.2 trillion), 10.6 per cent of all jobs (334 million), and was responsible for creating one in four of all new jobs across the world.[1] Even though the sector shrank substantially after Covid, it has now nearly returned to pre-Covid levels. Relatively speaking, the global travel and tourism sector is about three times the Indian economy. Mathews had the choice to expand horizontally or vertically in the software industry. He chose the latter route, going deep into one sector globally. The fruits are there to see:

- fifteen of the twenty leading airlines in the world are IBS customers;
- IBS' iAirport©, an interactive web-based system for managing airport operations and terminal management, is being used by Heathrow Airport, London, among other airports;
- IBS offers management solutions for eighty prominent global hotel chains;
- 70 per cent of cargo movement at airports in Japan and Australia is managed by IBS Software Solutions; and
- as of 2023, IBS has a presence in about sixty countries.

Going forward, the digitalization and the technology component in travel and tourism can only increase. The business context is completely changing—the way we produce, the way we distribute, the way we consume on demand and the way we transact (cashless and in real time). Air travel, hospitality and holidaying, and airport management will increasingly be fuelled by digital transformation.

No wonder then that twenty-five years after IBS began its journey, its enterprise valuation today stands at roughly $2 billion. Its mindset and strategy of defining its focus to meet its purpose has helped IBS scale these heights and build an enduring corporation.

Dodla Dairy: Taking Balanced Risks

The dictionary meaning of 'risk' is exposure to danger or harm. Why would a family business owner expose his or her company to danger? Because achieving scale cannot happen with a mindset of being in a comfort zone. Taking risks is unavoidable for scaling; however, it is important to take calculated, balanced risks. That's exactly what Sunil Reddy of Dodla Dairy did. The specific strategy of risk employed by Reddy was a judicious combination of organic and inorganic growth: acquisitions and greenfield plants.

The first and parent dairy plant of Dodla Dairy started in 1997 in Nellore with an investment of about Rs 8 crore. About three years later, it acquired a plant in Chittoor at a cost of about Rs 40 lakh. This was not an easy decision to make because the company had not touched overall profitability and there was a high debt repayment obligation as the capital expenditure loan taken from IDBI Bank was to be repaid with a 24 per cent rate of interest in five years.

Says Sunil Reddy, 'It was a very difficult decision for us. But once the team was able to take a call and acquire the plant, and the asset came into play, the Rs 40 lakh asset gave us a return of about Rs 1.5 crore. This was one of the best ways for us to scale-up at that point of time.' This was during the company's early days. It helped that it was not a public limited company and that there were no investor pressures or direction. That was a counter-intuitive strategy, because, normally in the early days of any company when it is struggling financially, it tends to be risk-averse and conservative in its growth ambitions. But what Reddy did was to take a balanced, calculated risk with the acquisition. It paid off.

Along with this calculated risk, after the takeover of the plant, the management brought in financial discipline and cost-saving measures. It was a loss-making plant and it had to be turned around. This proved to be a blessing in disguise because the need for discipline was like a financial handcuff. With all these measures, in a few years, the company turned around.

The company believes that debt-based acquisition is sometimes better than even bringing in private equity. A few years ago for instance, when the going was good, the company acquired KC Dairy for over Rs 100 crore. Reddy and the management were able to turn around that company too. Mastering turnaround after taking over sick companies is an art that the Dodla Group has perfected. It brings down the risks involved. Today, the company is cash surplus, but it is the mindset of taking risks at the right time and not being too conservative that has brought Dodla Dairy to where it is today.

An important element of Dodla's scaling mindset and strategy has been its ability to combine organic and inorganic growth. It has also perfected the art of setting up efficient and cost-effective greenfield plants. Reddy does this by getting the entire team galvanized towards a single focus of completing the project in record time. One recent example was a new dairy plant in Hyderabad set up at a cost of about Rs 100 crore. Building a greenfield plant requires patience and perseverance. There is a lot of effort that goes into buying the land, getting permissions, putting up the building and getting the machinery. Compared to this, acquiring a plant at a premium is much easier. However, that also has its challenges in getting the synergies into place.

The mindset of balanced risk has ensured that despite Dodla Dairy's worth (about Rs 3,000 crore) and being about twenty-five years in the business, it has not ventured into any unrelated investments. What it has done instead is to expand its product categories within dairy, which now is quite expansive and includes milk, curd, ice cream, milk-based sweets, butter, ghee and paneer. As of now, it is only in the business that it knows well and believes it can succeed in. To that extent, Reddy says they are old school entrepreneurs.

Expert Take by M.S.A. Kumar

Joan of Arc said, 'All battles are first won or lost in the mind.' There is another saying, 'Battles are never lost in the battlefield; but in the minds of the soldiers who fight the battle.' The same is the case with some business owners. Maintaining the status quo and sticking to one's comfort zone are two avoidable mindsets. Chapter 4 on strategy covers this aspect—of whether the vision, the goal, defines actions (jaise lakshya, vaise karma) in all cases, or not—in detail.

According to renowned American psychologist Carol Dweck, those who possess growth mindsets are more likely to be successful. A growth mindset stimulates one's drive, willingness and overall foundation of belief, to achieve bigger and better outcomes, so essential for longevity and scaling. On the contrary, according to Dweck, those having a fixed mindset believe their capabilities, qualities and traits are permanent and cannot be developed through time. Therefore, they tend to avoid failure at all costs and are conservative—sticking to comfort zones in other words.

The three examples—Eastern Condiments (thinking big), IBS Software Solutions (staying focused) and Dodla Dairy (willing to take balanced risks)—are pointers to the criticality of a business leader's mindset in driving longevity, growth and scale. A leader's mindset makes all the difference. There is a saying: to check whether a fish has gone bad, look at the gills in fish's head. If the gills are red, it means the fish is good to eat. Similarly, to know whether the organization is good to scale and grow, look at the leader's mindset.

One experience I would like to share is that of a family business owner who mentioned, 'I have two factories and my two smart sons are managing the same well. I want to put up a third factory in the neighbouring state. I don't have a third son to look after the factory!' The owner hadn't professionalized the business to depute his best manager to the third location. This mindset case is one of inability to take risks in business. The business stagnated with growth limited to price increases due to cost push; no volume or market share growth. But the patriarch was a happy person!

In fact, many conflicts in family businesses have their origins in the differing mindsets of the family members. The son wants to bring in private equity to scale and grow, the father wants to retain control and doesn't entertain outsider interference, the elder brother is conservative, whereas the younger brother is aggressive and likes to take calculated risks. One way to tackle the differing mindsets of family members is to align them to a common direction through a workshop on vision, mission and values. Though one has a growth mindset, finding the required resources to grow is the challenge that needs an open mind to tap resources lying outside the business.

4

STRATEGY

The Vision–Action Connection: Jaise Lakshya, Vaise Karma?

When Dhirajlal (Dhirubhai) Ambani left Aden (Yemen) in 1958 at the age of thirty-six to start a partnership firm, Majin, in Mumbai, and later, Reliance Commercial Corporation in 1966, it is said that he did so without any long-term vision beyond that of a small firm. Today, the diversified Indian multinational is the country's largest company by revenue and the largest publicly-traded enterprise by market capitalization with interests in petrochemicals, energy, retail, telecommunications, mass media and textiles.

It is largely believed that if a family business' founder has a clear and lofty vision to scale and grow, then it will happen. But

Ambani turned this much-trusted axiom—there is a strong and direct connection between vision and action (i.e., jaise lakshya, vaise karma)—on its head. He thought and started small. His vision evolved with time, and was taken forward by his eldest son Mukesh Ambani to stretch the limits.

The above iconic example shows us that there is a mixed record on this front.

Founder of Eastern Condiments M.E. Meeran too was not driven by any grand vision but by a passion for entrepreneurship and a yearning for a better quality of life, which prompted him to leave his native village, Nellimattom, for the more conducive and strategically located Adimali where he set up a small shop called Eastern Coffee and Curry Powder, in 1961.

On the other hand, Aravind Eye Care System founder Dr V had a crystal-clear vision when he set up the first Aravind Eye Hospital in the South Indian temple town of Madurai, in 1976. His vision was to eradicate preventable blindness as far as possible. Thus, while Eastern Condiments was able to scale through an evolutionary process, the Aravind Eye Care System grew through a set of radical actions emanating out of a purpose, executed with laser-sharp focus. '*Jaise lakshya, vaise karma*' is therefore not mandatory for super success stories.

Choosing a Strategy

The term 'strategy' became part of popular management terminology when Professor Michael Porter famously defined it as 'deliberately choosing a different set of activities to deliver a unique mix of value'. While there are a host of strategies to achieve scale and longevity, we will discuss three—positioning, purpose, and partition—that are very relevant in building lasting organizations, citing the example of four out of our twelve case studies.

Evolve Back Resorts: Positioning-Driven

George Ramapuram, MD, Evolve Back Resorts, is also its chief architect. He has travelled extensively, staying in some of the world's finest hotels, primarily to understand more about luxury hospitality and service.

For Evolve Back Resorts, positioning it at the top in the super-luxury segment was not just a thought-through choice but also part of the family's DNA. George Ramapuram says that the family always loved the best that life had to offer. Younger sibling Jose Ramapuram avers that their father 'Sunny' Thomas Ramapuram, who was progressive and prosperous right from his younger days, instilled in them the art of fine living. Says Jose, 'There was no market study done with regard to our positioning, but ultimately it has worked out really well.'

Solid business reasons also counted for positioning the resorts at the upper end. Lower profitability and greater competition at the lower segments were two of the reasons to stay away from this segment. Evolve Back pricing was intentionally kept 40 to 50 per cent above the nearest competition in each destination, and the number of rooms fewer than the competition, to maintain the exclusivity and personalized service. Its business model is: low-volume, high value. By positioning resorts at the luxury aspirational end, it goes without saying that Evolve

Back's profitability levels are high and this allows them to invest further into their infrastructure with minimal long-term debt and working capital loans from banks. This is a good strategy for scaling in a niche segment.

Says George Ramapuram, 'Luxury is all about being original, being with nature, with minimum disturbance to other people and nature. Fortunately, this is in line with the overall philosophy of Ramapuram Holdings.'

George recounts how they learnt from experience. Many years back, George and Jose went to meet a reclusive French billionaire and his wife who were guests at their resort at Hampi. They noticed that he rarely went out of his room and even when he did, he travelled in a limousine to take in the beautiful ruins of Hampi. It made George think deeply about the psyche and mind of the rich and famous. Evolve Back's philosophy is built on such observations. Today Evolve Back has super-premium private pool suites/villas at all their resorts, designed to provide complete privacy, peace and quiet. Guests enjoy sitting in their private veranda under the starry sky, taking in the sounds of crickets, night birds and frogs. George says that their experience shows that an increasing number of their guests are looking for an exclusive space, want solitude with nature and do not mind paying high rates. A natural corollary for Evolve Back and its luxury strategy is its mission statement: 'Providing exquisite holiday experiences while preserving the purity of nature and culture of the land.'

This is so crucial to them that it is also captured in their tag line: 'spirit of the land'. This is the second pillar of its positioning strategy. The spirit of the destination or the 'localness' is captured and showcased in luxury at each of their four destinations: Coorg, Kabini and Hampi in India, and Kalahari in Botswana. This also helps Evolve Back differentiate itself from other brands.

How do they do it? When Hampi was decided as a new destination, George Ramapuram, Evolve Back MD and chief architect, went with his team, studied the history, architecture, culture and lifestyles of the local people and incorporated them into the experiences and architecture of the Hampi resort. That is also the reason why the Hampi resort—the Evolve Back Kamalapura Palace—is built in the Vijayanagara dynasty palace style. The resort captures the spirit of Hampi in all its vividness.

Evolve Back's business model and strategy are built around the philosophy of maintaining a fine balance between a successful and profitable business, a great experiential holiday for its customers, a healthy environment and a prosperous local community. We learn from the company that not surprisingly, 90 per cent of the customers who stay at Evolve Back resorts are high-networth individuals and families from Indian and foreign urban centres. Celebrity guests include Nandan Nilekani, Azim Premji, Rahul Dravid, L.K. Advani, Lord Chris Patten (the last British governor general of Hong Kong), and Gita Gopinath (deputy MD, International Monetary Fund [IMF]). High-end and celebrity guests draw in others of a similar profile. Aspiration is the name of the game.

Overall, this is a very evolved and unique business model which is difficult to replicate. At the same time, once you master the model within a business group, it is a sure-fire strategy for scale and success.

Aravind Eye Care System: Purpose-Driven

'Purpose' as strategy is a supremely mature concept. In the case of Aravind Eye Care System, it is also a multidimensional concept that encompasses vision, sacrifice, excellence, spirituality and togetherness among many other things.

In 1976, Dr Venkataswamy (Dr V) brought together his immediate and extended family and set up the first Aravind Eye Hospital, with the express vision to prevent needless blindness and vision impairment in the world. Today, globally, at least 2.2 billion people have a near or distance vision impairment. In at least a billion, or almost half of these 2.2 billion cases, vision impairment could have been prevented or has yet to be addressed. The leading causes of vision impairment and blindness are uncorrected refractive errors and cataracts. The majority of people with vision impairment and blindness are over the age of fifty, living in low- and middle-income countries.

It is estimated that India is home to a third of all the blind people in the world. The problem of rapidly escalating avoidable blindness remains a major cause of concern in the Indian healthcare landscape. In a developing country like India, the government alone cannot meet the health needs of all owing to a number of challenges like growing population, inadequate infrastructure, low per capita income, aging population, diseases in epidemic proportions and illiteracy.

Realizing this, Dr V wished to establish an alternate healthcare model that could supplement the efforts of the government and also be self-supporting. In 1976, following his retirement at the age fifty-eight, he established the GOVEL Trust under which

Aravind Eye Hospitals were founded. The hospitals are named after Sri Aurobindo, one of the twentieth century's most revered spiritual leaders. In essence, Sri Aurobindo's teachings focused on transcendence to a heightened state of consciousness and becoming better instruments for the divine force to work through.

In the first Aravind Eye Hospital, with eleven beds and four medical officers under him, Dr V saw the potential for what is today one of the largest facilities in the world for eye care. Over the years, this organization has evolved into a sophisticated system dedicated to compassionate service for sight. The Aravind model is about affordability. Fifty per cent of its patients receive services either free of cost or at steeply subsidized rates, yet the organization remains financially self-sustainable. Much importance is given to equity—ensuring that all patients are accorded the same high-quality care and service, regardless of their economic status. When you combine affordability and scale with excellence, it is a potent combination.

Dr V, watching a tennis match on television, once asked Dr Kim (family member and presently chief medical officer [CMO] and director IT & Systems) why Martina Navratilova was playing so well. Dr Kim answered that she was very good because she had been playing for a long time. Dr V added, 'The only thing that makes a difference is she is practicing. She is trying to excel herself. So, we should have our doctors do their clinical work so well that they become excellent.' Says Dr Kim, 'These motivational conversations and such thinking is what brings many of us into the Aravind fold and keeps us there. In fact, the challenge amongst us is how each one of us in the family is able to consistently do much better, day by day, year by year.'

Another critical component of Aravind's model is its high patient volume, which brings with it the benefits of economies of scale. Aravind's unique assembly-line approach increases productivity tenfold. As of March 2023, over 7,00,000 eye surgeries or procedures are performed per year (2022-23) at Aravind, making it the largest eye-care provider in the world. Since its inception, Aravind has handled more than 7.8 crore (78 million) outpatient visits and performed more than 94 lakh (9.4 million) surgeries.

Aravind is unique in that it is a non-profit organization, promoted and largely led by the founding family members who number over thirty, now into the third generation. Says ED Operations R.D. Thulasiraj, 'The north star or the glue that is keeping us together involves quite a few things. But I think the most important is our purpose, which focuses on eliminating needless blindness. This requires a certain business model wherein you are inclusive, you are serving the poor, have high efficiency. Internally also, in order to reduce dependency on external funding we had decided not to raise any donations for running the institution. This had to be done through internal financing. That was one part of it. And the other part is the way the hospitals are organized. That also reinforces both the purpose as well as the value framework.'

What started off as an eleven-bedded hospital has now become a conglomerate, the Aravind Eye Care System. Today, the group operates a growing network of eye-care facilities, a postgraduate institute, a management training and consulting institute, an ophthalmic manufacturing unit, a research institute and eye banks. Its eye-care facilities include fourteen eye hospitals, six outpatient eye-examination centres and 108 primary eye-care facilities. Aravind Eye Care System now serves as a model for India and the rest of the world: a perfect example of scalability through purpose-driven strategy.

Eastern Condiments and IBS Software: Partnership-Driven

Eastern Condiments: To start with M.E. Meeran's sons, Navas and Firoz set long-term goals on multiple fronts: having a pan-India presence, a diversified product portfolio, and building world-class systems and processes. Navas, the older of the two by fifteen years and who joined the business first, has a mindset of growth and expansion. He understood that to grow he needed to bring in technology, funding and global-standard auditing. All three were done through partnerships—Deloitte in auditing, and McCormick and Orkla in funding. Navas is ambitious and a forward-thinker and used partnerships as a strategy for growth and scale. This is something that many MSME family businesses can learn.

Partnerships as a strategy for growth and scale is not new. But quite often they fail or do not achieve their intended goals. However, Eastern Condiments and the trio of M.E. Meeran and his sons, Navas and Firoz, perfected the art of successful partnerships and struck pure gold.

Eastern's revenue tripled to Rs 900 crore after the strategic tie-up with McCormick & Co. in 2010. Today, Eastern produces an eclectic range of products, which, apart from spices and blends, include masalas, pickles, tea, coffee, ethnic cuisine mixes and ready-to-cook varieties.

The latest step, its merger with Norway's Orkla ASA, aims to forge a professional partnership in Eastern's race towards becoming over Rs 72 billion ($1 billion) company by capitalizing on the increasing growth in the food industry in the next five to ten years. Orkla's Indian subsidiary MTR, and Eastern can now come out with a bouquet of products to tempt any refined palate.

Says Navas, 'Apart from the equity that Orkla has brought, we have benefited through multiple learnings, prominent among them being board management and the standard operating procedures. This partnership has helped professionalize Eastern and make it world-class.' Sums up Firoz, 'An important reason why this partnership has been successful is that we decided to run Eastern and MTR as two full-fledged entities rather than merge into one. There are many knowns and unknowns and having the flexibility is very useful. At the same time, Orkla's global game is to be fully local.'

IBS Software: India has access to technology and technologists, but does not have the business domain competency required to play at a global level, especially if a company wants to be at the leading edge of creating or designing technology solutions. Hence acquisition for acquiring capability was a strategy that IBS used.

It acquired a company in Switzerland in 2002 to get capability for flight operations and a company in 2003 in the UK, from Honeywell Corporation, that has given it the capability in airport operations. In 2005, IBS acquired a company in Washington DC called Discovery Travel Systems, which gave it capability in the travel, especially cruise, sector. In 2008, it acquired two companies—one in Boston called Biz-air Inc., which specializes in aircraft maintenance engineering; and the second in Atlanta, called Hotel Booking Solutions Incorporated (HBSi), which gave

IBS capability in the hospitality/hotels sector. More recently, in 2019–20, IBS took over a company called Adopt Systems in Canada, Montreal. The UK acquisition and the Canada acquisition were relatively bigger acquisitions that have created a centre of excellence within IBS for flight optimization.

Says founder V.K. Mathews, 'Acquisition was unusual for Indian companies then. Very few Indian companies would have gone outside and acquired other companies. It always used to be the reverse. But IBS started doing this at a very early stage. That was also a very clear path for us since we wanted to be vertically focused. The domain know-how is important. What we have in India in abundance is the technology and technologists. But we don't have the domain sophistication. You might have domain but we don't have the domain sophistication as yet. We believed that if we took a small vertical or area, then we could make a difference. Mergers and acquisitions, alliances, collaborations and partnerships make up our strategy to achieve that end.'

Mathews used partnership as a strategy to bring in private equity investments as well, first from General Atlantic (in 2007) and then from Blackstone (in 2015, which picked up General Atlantic's stake in IBS). With this sale, General Atlantic made 'more than twice its investment made in 2007 in the company'.[1] Adds Mathews, 'The Blackstone investment not only brought in capital but also helped us in opening doors globally.'

Expert Take by M.S.A. Kumar

When we explored the vision–action connection—jaise lakshya, vaise karma—we saw that some family business patriarchs, such as the late M.E. Meeran or for that matter late Dhirubhai Ambani, did not start with a stated strategy, goal or a lofty vision at the outset. The growth and scaling of their businesses evolved as they identified new business opportunities and moved nimbly to tap them. The three Ps (positioning, purpose and partnerships) have been demonstrated by Eastern Condiments, Evolve Back, Aravind, and IBS. These four case studies show clearly how the three Ps have helped in building trans-generational, long-lasting successful family businesses.

On the other hand, a clearly articulated vision statement as in the case of Aravind 'to eliminate needless blindness' enabled the large family to bond and work together to the actualize the vision of Dr Venkataswami.

In my experience as an as advisor to family businesses, I have observed that vision supported by mission (the purpose) and a long-term strategic business plan, minimizes conflict and differences of opinion among family members, because everybody commits to what the organization should accomplish in the long term.

If you look at Eastern to start with, Navas and Firoz worked on multiple long-term goals: a pan India presence, a diversified product portfolio, and world-class systems and processes. Navas has a mindset of growth and expansion. He had set a goal for Eastern to grow. That was the number one difference. Secondly, he understood that to scale, he needed to bring in technology, funding and global standards of account keeping and auditing. All three of the above were done through partnerships: McCormick for technology and private equity in funding, and Deloitte in auditing. Navas is ambitious and a forward thinker and used partnerships as a strategy for growth and scale. This is something that many MSME family businesses can learn to do.

At a broader level, the concept of jaise lakshya, vaise karma is relevant at two levels. Sometimes, the vision–action connection has provided the foundation for success, at other times a layered foundation was built through evolution. For example, in the case of the Eastern group, it was only after M.E. Meeran's sons, Navas and Firoz, came into the company that ambition, vision and money (that led to scale and growth) became important. The next generation led the charge of scale.

Clearly, vision and strategy are two pillars of scale.

5
GOVERNANCE
Managing the Family and the Business

'STRONG FAMILY GOVERNANCE CAN CREATE AN environment of smooth decision-making, cohesiveness, effective conflict-resolution and a direction that moves the business forward. Strong governance is critical to taking families from one generation of success to the other. Family business governance helps maximize family and business potential.'[1] You cannot have greater clarity on the importance of family business governance than this. Coming as it does from perhaps the world's foremost family business guru Professor John L. Ward, it is not surprising.

Although family business governance has been in vogue in India's large family conglomerates for more than a quarter of a century since liberalization in 1991, its gradual and sometimes reluctant acceptance by MSMEs has been observed for just about a decade or so. The push for raising the bar on governance, however, was triggered not only by heightened market competition and globalization but also by the growing trend of fratricidal wars in family businesses in the late 1980s and '90s. The ugly spats in Reliance, spats among the Shrirams of DCM, and in the Bajaj group were reminders that no business family, howsoever seemingly close or infallible, is immune to the destructive powers of division. In recent years, the entry of private equity and the need to unlock institutional value have also prompted governance in family businesses.

In such circumstances, strong governance systems and institutions to manage both the family and the business are critical. One of the most important objectives of governance in family businesses is to sustain peace, happiness and harmony in the family, which leads to longevity of the family, the business, and to greater stakeholder wealth creation and returns.

Over the years, many governance tools and techniques have been created the world over. Foremost among them are the family constitution, the family council, the family business board, an independent board of directors, advisory boards, a new charter for women, and family offices to manage intergenerational and long-term wealth. However, in implementing these, three important lessons stand out. (i) There cannot be a cookie-cutter approach, we need to customize each governance solution for every business family, though broad templates of governance can exist. (ii) We need flexibility while creating these mechanisms. (iii) Personal egos have no place, while humility and sacrifice among family members remain paramount requirements, even when there are written agreements.

High-quality governance mechanisms are a prerequisite for scaling-up.

The Meerans and the Ramapurams: Family Constitution

Conventional wisdom in today's business world suggests the importance and need for a family constitution for those with a family business. But our own experience and interactions with other family business owners suggest that a family constitution is deeply contextual and dictated by the size, complexity and the stage of life-cycle of the family business.

The Rs 1,800 crore Group Meeran (Eastern Condiments) does not have a family constitution, though the family realizes its importance. One main reason for smooth functioning, despite the absence of a written family constitution, is that siblings Navas and Firoz Meeran are very close to each other and aligned to the values that their father has engendered in them. In the second generation, their go-slow on creating a constitution is also because they have come up from humble beginnings and are acutely aware of the grace they have received as a family.

Says Navas, 'When we create a constitution, it may not always be business-friendly. For example, if the family is small and has a clause that a brother-in-law cannot be part of it, but if there is a financial emergency and he wants to help out, it cannot be that the constitution prohibits his participation. Business growth and not strict rules should be the primary focus of a family business.'

Adds Firoz, 'If you ask me whether a constitution is required or not, I would always vote for it, but with the caveat that it should be participative, flexible, open for review and non-bureaucratic. The family constitution should not curtail the entrepreneurial spirit of the business.' Today, Eastern Condiments is helped along by the fact that the third generation is yet to become fully active in the business, which is probably when they might feel the need for a family constitution.

On the other hand, the context completely changes in the House of Ramapuram. With the third generation fully involved in the business and the second generation of seven brothers moving towards retirement, there are today about thirty-five members from the family in the business and a family constitution is in place.

The Ramapurams began their search for a family business advisor who could help them draft a constitution, once the third generation entered the picture. The search continued apace but to no avail. Until one day when New Delhi-based Anil Sainani was well on his way to creating a family constitution for the Bengaluru-based group after a series of discussions with the family members. Today, they live and breathe the constitution and swear by it.

Professor John Ward describes a family business constitution as 'a comprehensive articulation of philosophy, principles and policies for the future that balances and synthesizes the welfare of family, owners and the business, [and] is among the most important steps a business-owning family can take to secure and strengthen its business and, most preciously, its family.'[2]

A constitution can take various forms depending on the family, its business, its stage of development, and the preferences of family members. It can be a concise document or a detailed and intricate one. Generally, a constitution fulfils the following primary purposes:

1. it records the family's mission, values, philosophy, and principles that guide their business, including the challenges faced by previous generations;
2. it outlines the business's strategy, long-term and short-term goals, and the steps needed to achieve them;
3. it defines the processes for resolving disputes that may arise and affect the business and the family, and ensures that conflicts are managed and resolved in a fair and timely manner;
4. it describes how the key governing and other groups within a business—such as management, directors, shareholders, and family members—are organized, and also their responsibilities, make-up, and the authority they hold; and,
5. the shareholder agreement is an attachment to the constitution.

The family constitution covers various crucial aspects such as compensation, lifestyle needs, entry requirements for the next generation, retirement planning, education of children, and ensuring the security of wives after their spouse passes away. Additionally, the constitution also addresses succession planning both within and between generations.

A family constitution is typically a written document that all family members involved in a business review acknowledge and sign, but it is not usually a legally-binding agreement. Instead, it creates a moral obligation signifying each family member's commitment to preserving the family's legacy and growing the business for future generations. To ensure objectivity, most families engage an outside advisor to lead and drive the process and possibly serve as a referee.

The family constitution should be a working, flexible document that can adapt to changing times and circumstances, and it should be regularly reviewed and updated. Any changes made to the constitution should align with its original intent and goals, and changes should only be made when necessary. It is contextual to the family how often changes are made, and the time gap should be discussed and agreed upon by family members.

The Geras: Composing a Board of Directors

A strong and vibrant board of directors raises the standards of governance, which in turn makes a definitive contribution to a company's growth. Gera Developments is a textbook case of far-sighted and high-quality board composition and management. With shareholding closely held within the family, it boasts of three much-respected, non-family, names of India Inc. on its advisory board: Deepak Parekh of HDFC, Farhad Forbes of Forbes Marshall Ltd and Baba Kalyani of the (Bharat Forge) Kalyani Group of Companies.

Despite their high stature, all three have been on the board of Gera Developments, a relatively smaller company, for seven years and have been advising the company on a pro-bono basis. Kalyani is a fellow Pune resident and they are family friends and along with their spouses they often meet for dinner or other informal get-togethers such as on birthdays, where they discuss work along with personal interests. Hotel Conrad Pune is a favourite haunt. The power of hard work is what Kumar Gera has observed and learnt from Kalyani.

Kumar and the management team go to these external directors every quarter or as needed and share their plans and in turn, receive valuable feedback. For example, Deepak Parekh, a visionary with great insights on numbers, in a recent board meeting, told Rohit Gera who had taken over as the CEO that HDFC considers Gera Developments high up on the integrity index among the country's real estate developers. Therefore, his advice to the company would be that based on this foundation, Gera Developments should focus on building its brand.

Says Kumar Gera, 'Basically, he directed us towards building and protecting the brand. Now the question is, when you want to build the brand of a company what all do you have to do? One has to go into that and I think that was a very good direction to move into. It wasn't a numbers game; it wasn't about your bottom line. It wasn't about any one particular thing. When you look at how a brand gets built, you have to have a good product and more. So, all these things in a very simple message were conveyed by Deepak.' Beyond the boardroom, informal advisors and mentors have also influenced Gera Developments and Kumar Gera. Rahul Bajaj is one of them and Kumar says he is fortunate to have learnt from Rahul about forthrightness, truth, plain speaking and attention to detail.

The lesson: a formal high-quality board of directors and an equally high-profile informal set of advisors is a potent mix that aids scaling-up of family business MSMEs.

The core of a company's corporate governance practice is its board of directors, which is responsible for safeguarding the interests of stakeholders and ensuring their health and security. In addition to promoting the company's strategic thinking and executing plans with sincerity, the board also fosters ethical behaviour and establishes conditions that promote relationship-building and learning. A robust corporate bureaucracy structure and a competent board comprising of insightful individuals are essential for good corporate strategy and performance.

What, then, makes a great board? Five important dimensions.

1. An independent and open-minded board that possesses relevant expertise and diversity provides valuable insights on business strategy and performance and acts as a sounding board for management. It is crucial to select board members of stature who are respected by management and are willing to listen to bad news. Independent directors with diverse backgrounds, expertise, and professional experience play a central role in strategic governance and growth of a firm, regardless of its size.
2. A well-functioning board engages in detailed planning for board meetings, including sending necessary information to board members at least two weeks prior to the meeting.

This practice enables the board to concentrate on crucial discussions and decisions during the meeting, rather than simply reviewing numbers and presentations.

3. Having an appropriate number of non-executive independent directors—who provide advisory services, bring their reputation and networks, and serve on various committees such as audit, compensation, investor grievance, nominations, and risk management—is crucial for bringing valuable perspectives to the company. These directors offer diverse and independent viewpoints, which help improve decision-making processes, enhance transparency, and promote good corporate governance.
4. In a family business, the promoter family is typically the dominant shareholder. However, when multiple family members are actively involved in the business, a good board ensures that decision-making is based on what is best for the enterprise rather than for any particular individual or group within the family. This helps to maintain objectivity and prevent conflicts of interest that could otherwise undermine the company's success.
5. A great board is not a mere rubber stamp for decisions already made by management, nor is it simply focused on governance. Instead, it actively contributes to the company's strategy, manages risks effectively, enhances decision-making processes, and leads for the long-term. In the past, board members often functioned as rubber stamps for the family. However, in the current era, some strong corporate managements may consider their decisions to be a fait accompli. A great board is able to challenge such management

decisions and provide valuable feedback that benefits the company's overall performance and sustainability.

In our experience, we have noticed the reluctance of the family business patriarch to have outsiders on the statutory board. The main reason is the family members don't easily accept reviews/critical comments by an outsider. They want absolute freedom to decide during the board meetings—a misplaced notion of losing control! On the other hand, to get good independent directors in the statutory board is also a challenge, given the amendments in the Companies Act, 2013, regarding the accountability of independent directors. What is the way out? As a starting point, we recommend the formation of an advisory board without fiduciary responsibilities.

The Datlas: Gender and Women Empowerment

Vanitha Datla hailed from the famous Raasi Group of erstwhile Andhra Pradesh. Inspired by her doctor father, she wanted to be a doctor and tried her best to gain admission in a medical school. Those days there were limited seats in the state and when she failed to gain a seat in the merit quota, she pleaded with her family for a seat in a neighbouring state with a capitation fee. Of course, as is expected, they refused, not wanting to send her out of the state and ensured that she got married at the earliest. Her dream died and she moved unhappily to pursue a Bachelor of Arts in a women's college in Hyderabad. She feels that if she had a mentor those days she could have at least pursued a course in the sciences stream as she was pretty good in life sciences.

Her grandfather, the patriarch of the family, had three daughters, all of whom had children. Her mother was the eldest daughter. The sons-in-law were already involved in the business group and the grandsons were getting formally groomed to be future business leaders. His companies in the cement, refractory and ceramics businesses were traditionally male dominated and had a miniscule percentage of women working in them. Vanitha always had an ambition to work, but never felt that she would enter the world of family business.

She married Ramesh Datla of ELICO at a very early age, while she was an undergraduate and later moved with him to the United States, discontinuing her education. Here, she gained the perspective that one could work anywhere and in any field, not necessarily restricted to one's dreams. She secured a job as a personal assistant to an insurance agent. Receiving a salary inspired her and made her aware of the importance of being financially independent. She would until then have had to ask Ramesh or, before she was married, her parents, for money whenever she wanted something. Being dependent on someone for your financial needs is definitely not a good feeling she admits. However, on earning for herself, she felt liberated.

Though she attended university and later a community college, Vanitha was not able to complete her graduation in the United States and after she moved back to India she made it a point to finish her undergraduate studies through the distance mode. Her passion to work at something and not just be relegated to the home front pushed her to request her grandfather for a position in his group companies. As a young mother to two pre-schoolers, she knew that a full-time professional career would impact her parenting. Taking the situation into consideration, she concluded that it would be best to work for the family business, which would enable flexibility in her work schedules. Vanitha admits to feeling ill-suited to tackle the role as she didn't possess the necessary educational qualifications. She very well knew that her relationship to the owner got her the position but to continue in the role she would have to prove herself and earn the respect of her colleagues at the workplace. She enrolled for the full-time CFA-PGDBA (Chartered Financial Analyst and Post Graduate Diploma in Business Administration) at the ICFAI Business School, while working with her grandfather and much to the surprise of everyone including her class mates she graduated second in class with a silver medal and was also offered a job at a good financial services company even though she never sat for campus placements.

Reminiscing about her career she feels that her grandfather would have never dreamt that she sustained at the workplace for close to three decades. 'I think he may have thought it was just a passing phase for me and eventually I would hang up my boots after a short stint, having tasted the uncertainties and complexities of business life. This must have been one of the reasons for him to accept my request for a role and place me in a position that would neither impact the business nor create any problems for me.' 'If that generation had provided to young women the same preparation, would they not have risen to the same level as that of their male counterparts, or even higher?' she quizzes.

The role of women in a family business today can be best understood looking back from a historical perspective. Women's roles have evolved and matured in large measure only in recent years. Today including women in the family business is a strong aspect of governance. Their contributions definitely go a long way in contributing to scale and growth. The women in a family business could be the wife of the patriarch, sister, daughter or daughter-in-law. This is a far cry from the early years of Indian family businesses when they were run by men and for men.

Although there have been some exceptions, women historically have faced challenges in heading family businesses. In the 1930s, for example, Shanti Kumar Morarji, leader of the Morarji Group, committed suicide after the business collapsed. His son was not interested in taking over the business, leaving his daughter-in-law to take charge. Despite initial reluctance, she successfully turned the business around. Simone Tata, a European woman who married into the influential Tata family, also set up a successful cosmetics company called Lakmé. However, after Ratan Tata took charge of the Tata Group, he sold the company. The increasing role of women in family businesses in India is partly due to family planning initiatives that began in the 1960s, which led to a shift toward smaller nuclear families with fewer boys. However, this change was not always easy, as traditional attitudes and cultural norms often favoured men over women in leadership roles. Despite these challenges, more and more women are taking on leadership positions in family businesses today.

To enter a family business, women leaders may consider starting small and focusing on areas of the business that they find interesting. They can then increase their involvement and take on more responsibilities. Having a mentor or coach can also be helpful. Women need to be proactive and step up, rather than remaining in the shadows. Achieving work–life balance is a challenge, despite the support of the family ecosystem. Women are often burdened with additional responsibilities that need to be balanced with their work commitments.

Decisions for succession, inheritance, choosing the next CEO or board member should be based on capabilities, interests and willingness instead of gender. Meritocracy over entitlement should be the guiding principle. Gradually, more and more women are joining the boards of companies but it is of equal importance that they are not rubber stamps. By nature, women are transformational leaders who can help transform people's self-interest into organizational goals. Women leaders are well equipped to be 'chief emotional officers' and 'chief trust officers' of the business. They have the ability to empathize and make everyone feel a part of the team. They are also capable of delivering tough messages but in ways that are more humane. Clearly, we need more Vanitha Datlas, Anu Agas and Lavanya Nallis.

Managing Conflict

Conflict is normal in human relationships, be it in business, or family, or family business. If well-managed, conflicts can be a catalyst for positive change/transformation. When a business scales up over two or three decades, the family running it also grows in number with GenNext ready to enter the management team. With the marriage of GenNext, spouses from a different background/culture join the family. Subsequent to marriage, families move from joint to nuclear. Thus, the family complexity changes significantly.

The location of different family members managing the business, also changes due to the geographical expansion of the business. Conflicts in family businesses can be on account of relationship matters or business matters or a combination of the two. The root cause of conflict is 'communication' with blotted egos doing the damage.

Here are some instances of communication in tough business and relationship matters:

> I get zero support from my father and elder brother. They don't listen to my new ideas to expand the business. They are very conservative.
>
> Thanks to my sister-in-law, my elder brother has become selfish. He wants to change the family understanding of same income for both of us.
>
> I want to sell my 30 per cent share in the family business. My uncle is not giving me a fair price nor is he allowing me to sell to a third party.
>
> Son: We have to change the business model, Dad, otherwise, we will soon be a BIFR company.[3]
>
> Dad: This is all part of the business cycle, son. Being young, you haven't gone through such ups and downs in business.

With the above starting points, conflicts can escalate to the destruction of the family business. Friedrich Glasl's 'conflict escalation model' is a very useful diagnostic tool for conflict resolution especially for sensitizing the family members involved.[4]

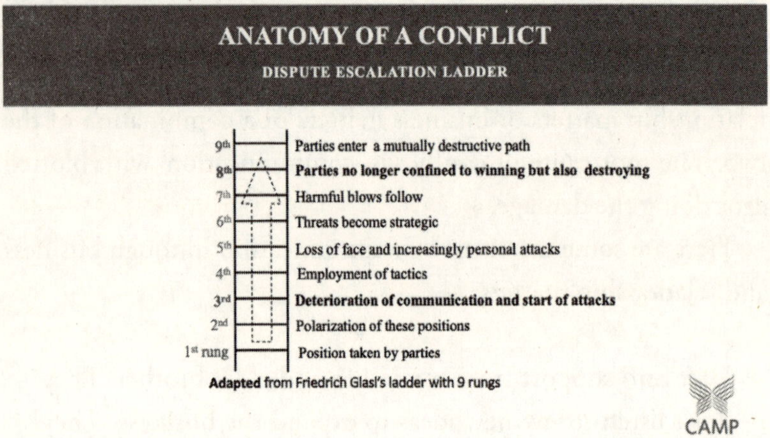

Source: CAMP Mediation

Prevention is always better and can be done through well-defined protocols for settling differences in a family constitution. The role of a family business advisor or a mediator may be called for, in resolving conflict if the conflict has gone beyond Stage 2 in the escalation ladder. This aspect is detailed in Chapter 13 ('Outsiders as Insiders'). In any case, early-stage detection and treatment is the best, whether medically or in business.

House of Anita Dongre: The Family Office

The institution of a family office serves as the keeper of a family's legacy, values, and constitution, and can take on different forms:

such as a single office that caters to one family with a large and complex business, or a multi-office that manages the affairs of multiple families. Each family office is distinct as it is influenced by factors such as the family's business, history, commercial and personal characteristics. The work and direction of the family office is purpose- and value-driven. Taking simple living to a high level, the family office aims to look after the genuine needs of the family members like the education of the younger generation, and also impact investing that will help preserve and grow the family's wealth over generations.

The family office as a wealth-preservation instrument is a relatively new but growing concept. The House of Anita Dongre decided to set up its family office shortly thereafter. The head of the family office of the House of Anita Dongre is Anita's soft-spoken, thirty-something nephew, Deepikesh Hira. With a sharp mind, a flair for numbers, and an eye for people and investments that will benefit the organization in the long term, Deepikesh spends a typical day scanning for impact investing opportunities, talking to family wealth advisors and learning about other family businesses in India and overseas that look towards intergenerational family wealth management.

Growing up in the eighty-three-island archipelago of Bahrain in the Persian Gulf, Deepikesh moved to Bengaluru and to Mumbai for his higher studies before joining the family business in 2010. After heading and driving group business development for five years, he joined the ISB, Hyderabad, studying the family business course, which equipped him with the fine art of managing the family's diverse businesses.

In early 2021, as the group moved into professionalization and growth, a collective call was taken to set up a group family office. Says Deepikesh, 'I felt it would suit my temperament. I enjoy meeting people and especially entrepreneurs and spending time with them. I also enjoy investing. Which is why I felt that it would suit my personality and this is why I opted to come in and join the family office. A lot of my time currently is focused on meeting entrepreneurs and trying to understand the lay of the land. We want to make sure that we are backing the right people and the right businesses.'

The thrust of the family office is to work in two interesting areas: (i) businesses that work towards the prevention of cruelty to animals; and (ii) businesses that are environment-friendly. To this end the House of Anita Dongre has invested in a Bengaluru-based electric vehicle company.

As a company and as a brand, the House of Anita Dongre is completely leather-free. Deepikesh wants to support any business or organization that is helping towards removing animals from the economic system: companies working on alternate proteins, meat alternates, animal-milk alternates and leather alternates.

The primary responsibility of a family office is to create a strong plan for preserving wealth over the long term. This plan should consider both external factors, such as changes in politics or technology that can affect family wealth, as well as internal factors, such as the family's cash-flow needs, cost of living, and the transition of wealth between generations. By defining a clear mandate based on these factors, the family office can establish an effective governance structure.

In terms of actually putting this plan into action, there are various methods that can be used. For instance, a basic portfolio consisting of 60 per cent equities and 40 per cent bonds; or a more diversified endowment model similar to those used at Harvard and Stanford; or a complex 'all-weather' strategy that manages risks related to inflation and growth changes. While each strategy may perform better in different market conditions, they all rely on the same crucial element: diversification to minimize risk.

The importance of diversification is highlighted by the historical performance of different asset classes over the past century. While equities have generally provided higher returns than other asset classes across different regions and time periods, holding all assets in one equity can prove disastrous; for example, those who held German equities from 1910 to 1930 would have faced permanent loss of capital due to war and hyperinflation. A comprehensive long-term wealth preservation strategy should consider all potential outcomes, even rare but possible occurrences like these.

Additionally, family offices are increasingly investing in start-ups, with successful entrepreneurs mentoring and investing in young talent to grow their next generation and explore new areas of the economy. These investments are often based on meritocracy, with single-family offices hiring top talent and implementing clear objectives and processes. Wealth multiplication through exits is also a common goal, rather than solely investing for the long term.

Meeran Group: Philanthropy

The Meerans' philanthropy philosophy is based on the principle that just as small droplets of water make up a large ocean, ongoing small acts of kindness go on to make a big impact.

Ten dialysis machines have been donated to a clinic in Adimali, in honour of M.E. Meeran. The doctors at this clinic charge only Rs 10 per patient for a consultation and medicines, lab tests are provided at subsidized rates. Similarly, at the government hospital in Kochi, the Meerans and Eastern Condiments have contributed Rs 2.5 crore (of the total cost of Rs 4 crore) for a linear accelerator (Linac) radiotherapy machine for treatment of cancer. Typically, the cost per radiation per patient is Rs 1 lakh. But because the cost of the machine has been taken care of, the hospital provides radiation services free of cost to those who cannot afford it. Navas and Firoz have also contributed substantially to a cancer hospital coming up in Calicut.

The advantage with all the above initiatives is that poor patients can get free/low-cost treatment because the initial capital expenditure has been taken care of.

Apart from contributing to healthcare causes, the Meerans support education for the needy. The rationale is based on the advice given by the senior Meeran who used to say: do not give them fish, but teach them how to fish. An interesting exercise is the caring for the education of tribal girls who normally get married at the age of about 12 years when they get pregnant. With education, the girls are able to lead an educated, empowered and normal life. One such girl secured the first rank in the state law course entrance exam. Group Meeran also runs a full-fledged school in Adimali.

There has been an evolutionary process to the development of philanthropy at Group Meeran. For the first thirty years or so, it was done unofficially with contributions. However, as the company professionalized and scaled, audits were brought in. Besides, the government also stepped in making corporate social responsibility (CSR) mandatory in recent years. That way the impact is made more sustainable.

Says Navas, 'We haven't structured CSR as of now. The problem is that when you structure it, you make too much of noise. We don't generally believe in that. That is the reason why we do it in a very subtle manner. We feel that these are all things which we are naturally supposed to do and we should do it, but you can't blow your own trumpet out of it.'

Family business philanthropy is important for a variety of reasons—the impact it makes, its potential as an agent of change, its positive contribution to society and polity, its philosophical and religious underpinnings, its ability to give a better future to the coming generations and last but not the least, it gives a soul to institutions and individuals practicing philanthropy.

Important to both the family and the business in a family business, philanthropy bonds family members bringing them together towards a common purpose. It helps in long-term sustainability of the family through generations, transfers knowledge and ideas and builds a legacy. For the business, it builds its brand and reputation, contributes to tax planning and government regulations, builds bridges with the polity and helps in creating ties with external stakeholders such as the communities around which the business is located.

Family business philanthropy in India goes back to the 1900s when many of the early business families contributed to the Independence movement, with special focus on the Swadeshi movement. Several industrial leaders extended their financial support to leaders of the freedom struggle. Ghanshyam Das Birla's financial contributions to the Independence movement and Ardeshir Godrej's generous donation to the Tilak Fund were notable among these. Not surprisingly, these early family businesses are even today torchbearers of the family philanthropy tradition creating economic opportunities and wealth. The Tatas and the Murugappas pioneered charitable contributions to hospitals and schools and continue to make a deep impact. On an average, Tata Sons contributes a significant 8–14 per cent of its net profit every year for philanthropic activities through various arms of the Tata Trust.

In Indian philosophy, service to mankind is believed to bring God's blessings, and hence business families chose to directly supervise their philanthropic activities. Philanthropy was traditionally viewed as a selfless act of service to humanity and to God, leading many prominent families to encourage women to get involved. Non-working family members, particularly women, played an active role in philanthropic decision-making. While some members of the family were focused on creating economic wealth, others took on the responsibility of serving as trustees of the family's legacy by initiating philanthropic projects aimed at improving the lives of the underprivileged.

Modern philanthropic efforts are significant because they are designed to address current social issues and tackle their root causes. Contemporary business philanthropy focuses on raising awareness of environmental problems such as deforestation, water conservation, and global warming, as well as social issues such as female infanticide, discrimination against girls, and the spread of diseases like HIV-AIDS.

The evolution of philanthropy has paralleled recent changes in the economy, with the acceleration of economic development through liberalization and progressive economic policies. Philanthropy has become increasingly focused on efficiency and effectiveness due to larger funds, more strategic planning, a more professional approach and greater emphasis on measuring outcomes and impact. With rapid economic growth and globalization of knowledge and funding resources, philanthropy has emerged as a mainstream professional activity in India. Companies are now hiring top professionals to manage their philanthropic efforts.

Philanthropy has expanded beyond simply giving money away and is now focused on building skilled manpower in relevant areas. The use of metrics, strategic decision-making, and professional approaches to solve developmental issues has become increasingly important as more individuals enter the field. This has created greater opportunities for volunteers and donors, including a growing number of young people entering the non-profit and philanthropy sectors. Many companies now adopt a triple bottom-line approach to philanthropy and sustainability, emphasizing people, planet, and profits. Despite these changes, the fundamental premise of philanthropy, its motto of service, remains unchanged.

While philanthropy is still relatively new in India, there are indications that it has the potential to make a significant contribution towards building a better world for both current and future generations. By continuing to refine their strategies, processes, and resource allocation, businesses and families can work together to create a better understanding and application of trusteeship, leading to more organized and strategic philanthropic initiatives. This could result in greater synthesis and synergy in the meaning and relevance of philanthropy, ultimately leading to a more impactful and sustainable future.

Three primary models of philanthropy have emerged: CSR, individual/family foundations, and a hybrid model: the family-corporate partnership.

Corporate Social Responsibility: Currently, CSR is the most widespread type of charitable activity globally, but the extent of involvement and effort varies considerably among organizations. Many big companies have a department dedicated to social responsibility that not only strives to improve the conditions of the surrounding community but also focuses on promoting the welfare of employees and workers. This latter aspect is now considered as part of CSR by companies.

The majority of philanthropic endeavours are carried out in the local business area, primarily due to their immediate effect on nearby stakeholders. Companies with multiple locations usually engage in community development initiatives in as many business sites as possible.

Individual/family foundations: In the 1990s, as the Indian economy underwent a transformation, a new generation of corporate leaders emerged, such as those at Infosys and Wipro, who demonstrated a great interest in utilizing their wealth for social development. They have shown how best practices from the corporate and for-profit sectors can be transferred and leveraged in the non-profit sector, particularly in the field of philanthropy. Many of these individuals and their families have established their own private foundations for charitable giving. These entrepreneurs are mostly first- or second-generation family members.

A family foundation is broadly defined as a charitable organization managed by individuals with family ties and supported by donations from those individuals, their businesses, and other investment income. In these individual or family foundations, the promoters take an active role in developing strategies and often engage in micro-level activities, depending on their interests and availability.

Hybrid Model: Certain foundations may also adopt a hybrid model. In India, the family-corporate partnership is one of the most common models of philanthropy. As most Indian businesses are family-run, a separate charitable organization, in the form of a foundation or trust, is established. This is primarily funded by the business but often led by the business family.

These organizations also tend to form partnerships with similar-minded groups—whether local, national, or international—to receive aid and expertise sharing. The primary advantages of this model include greater accountability, knowledge exchange, talent acquisition, the ability to rapidly expand programmes, and external funding that brings in system and process optimization.

Expert Take by M.S.A. Kumar

Clearly laid-out ground rules for running the family and the business are a must for creating a successful trans-generational institution that meets the expectations of all stakeholders. Succession planning, be it management or wealth, is a key element along with a well-constituted statutory or advisory board. Though a family business constitution is a desirable tool to define roles, responsibilities, code of conduct, dos and don'ts, we don't consider it a must especially for small families. However, as the number of family members involved in managing the business increases, so does the business' complexity. In such cases a well-drafted and crafted constitution—with the participation of all family members (including those not involved in running the business), and supported by a family business advisor (on whom the family has the trust)—can be considered.

I was asked by a family business owner to draft a family constitution for his group. His first suggestion to me was to send the standard family business constitution template and he would do the rest by filling-in whatever was required. Such an approach will never work for two reasons: (i) a family constitution is prepared by the family and for the family with the involvement and buy-in of all members of the family; and (ii) each family is unique, so one size doesn't fit all.

A prerequisite for an effective governance system is the existence of an organizational structure with roles, responsibilities and accountability (including for family members) being well-defined, and robust systems and processes. A performance management system with SMART (specific, measurable, attainable, relevant and time-bound) goal-setting and performance-linked variable pay, is another key element.

6

MANAGING MULTIGENERATIONAL TRANSITION

Succeeding at Succession Planning

THE IMPORTANCE OF PLANNED SUCCESSION AS A precursor for growth and building a lasting institution cannot be overstated in a family business. Successfully passing the baton to the next generation is a goal for many family business leaders. It can also be a sound business move if the right steps are taken. Quite often it does not happen that way and is therefore a huge challenge for many family businesses in India.

There are various reasons why business groups fail to succeed in succession planning. For one, members of the senior generation refuse to let go even when formal family codes and family constitutions stipulate retirement ages. There are also situations when there are conflicts with regard to the vision and implementation of business strategies and plans.

Second, a key concern is how non-family personnel will receive a family successor. Perceptions of capabilities and nepotism in succession can undermine non-family employee commitment to the business and their continued participation in the firm. Non-family employees also often sense that family members have less accountability or responsibility than they do. Large differentiation in compensation between the younger generation members of the family and professionals sometimes demotivates the latter group.

Further, family firms should also demand more from aspiring successors. Longer hours and tougher assignments during the transition process can inspire confidence among non-family employees in the dedication of the successor. This can help reassure employees that a family successor is the right person for the job. The potential successor's success is further enhanced if a non-family leader can train and develop them. Here again, the role of advisors becomes important. This aspect is elaborated in Chapter 13, 'Outsiders as Insiders'. Finally, the process of succession in family groups is often not transparent and is implemented without enough time and preparation. This also creates mistrust and conflicts within organizations.

To overcome the above limitations and challenges, there are some best practices that family businesses can create and foster. These include: ensuring that there is no 'helicopter landing', instilling family values, fostering humility and family togetherness, and learning from the past.

Sandu Pharmaceuticals: No 'Helicopter Landing'

'Helicopter landing' is an informal term used in business communication, especially in a family business context. It refers to a situation where next-generation family members join the group at senior positions, to which they would normally not be entitled. Just as a helicopter lands vertically, these young family members are literally dropped from above. This is not a perfect setting and does not promote meritocracy. Mumbai-based Sandu Pharmaceuticals defied this trend and inducted young family members through a proper succession-planning exercise. The youngsters had to prove themselves outside before taking on more complex and leadership roles within the company.

Gargi Sandu, fourth-generation and eldest daughter of Shashank Sandu, graduated from Pune's Symbiosis Law School in 2018. A corporate lawyer, she joined the iconic Mumbai-based law firm Kanga & Co. and worked as an understudy to the firm's senior partner, Preeti Mehta. After working there for about thirty months, she joined the legal department of Sandu Pharma with the department's non-family professional as her boss.

Gargi says it was not an easy process. One of the main challenges she faced when she joined the family business in 2020, was working with the people there and getting to understand where they were coming from and for them to understand her perspective. 'Coming from the law firm, I was used to a fast-paced work culture. It was different here and was something I struggled with in the beginning,' she recalls. 'Additionally, as you know, while it is always good to deal with the family because they are very understanding, but at the same time, it gets a little difficult working with them because there are people who are stuck with certain processes or ideologies. I came from a point of view that when you need to take quick decisions on growth and scale, it should be done so with an entrepreneurial mindset of flexibility and alacrity. But at Sandu, there are many layers of decision-making.'

When she joined in 2020, the world was in the midst of the pandemic and there were many tight timelines with the additional pressure of a limited workforce. And since Sandu operated in the pharmaceutical domain, there was greater market demand for its products. In this environment, Gargi had a certain set of expectations of how sales could be met. But she had to give up on some of her expectations because many of professionals at Sandu had been working there for decades and were almost like family members; their opinion overruled her viewpoint.

Similarly, she had many ideas on how the company's presence on social media could be enhanced. Being a family member she thought that everyone would promptly get on board to execute all these ideas. Then she realized there was a process to be followed. That was the first thing that was explained to her. She could have great ideas but there was a process to be followed. Sometimes she would go to her father in frustration, who would tell her that there was a past instance when something had gone wrong in the execution of a similar idea.

The roots of this value system and its philosophy of humility go back to Gargi's grandfather, to whom she was very close. Some of these nuggets of wisdom from her grandfather included 'money saved is money gained' and 'health is wealth'. Accordingly, when

Gargi stayed as a student at the Symbiosis hostel for five years, she would switch off the fans and air-conditioners if there was no one in the room. Despite coming from a privileged background, while working in Kanga & Co. in Mumbai, she commuted by bus or train with her colleagues. Says Gargi, 'That daily forty-five-minute bus ride was such a great interaction to build close relationships and friendships, which is something that I will hold on to for the rest of my life.'

Gargi's younger brother Virajeet also joined Sandu at a level in consonance with his age and experience. Prior to joining the family business, he worked in the risk-advisory division of the Big Four audit and consulting firm, Deloitte, in Mumbai. There, he was under the tutelage of one of the partners who specialized in the banking and mutual-fund sectors. After a few years, Virajeet joined Sandu. Like Gargi, he too had no 'helicopter landing'. He practiced and incorporated system integration in Sandu, which was something he had learnt at Deloitte.

Says Virajeet, 'In Sandu it is still an unfinished task. We are in the process of understanding every single segment of the business that the system is going to run through. Being a very traditionally set business we did have a few automated processes at our manufacturing unit, at the distribution centres. But the problem is that we were partly system-driven in particular departments, which made it even more challenging to integrate three to four departments together.'

How did the Sandu family learn and inculcate best practices in the group? One way was the learnings at family business conferences at ISB, Hyderabad, which were attended by both Gargi and Virajeet.

The other way that learnings came to the younger generation, interestingly through a counter-intuitive practice, was by not mixing professional and personal life and keeping home relationships separate. Although the jury is still out on whether this is a good practice or not, at Sandu's they live by it. Virajeet, for example, calls his father Baba at home and Shashank Sir at work. Additionally, at the dinner table they never talk about business affairs. The Sandus believe that this distinction between personal and professional is important as it helps in professionalization and transparent succession planning. Being a family member does not grant that youngster any entitlement. He or she has to earn their stripes by merit. The source of these best practices stems from the classes that both Gargi and Virajeet learnt at ISB.

The Geras: Learning from the Past to Envision the Future

Practicing family togetherness and unity for business growth is not easy. Kumar Gera learnt this lesson the hard way. Even as Kumar took on more responsibility in the business, he remained subordinate to his father Pritamdas for twenty years. As he entered his late thirties, Kumar's frustration mounted. He had to walk the narrow line between questioning his father and doing what he believed was right for the business. At Gera, the hierarchy would remain intact until 1991, when Pritamdas fell ill and Kumar was forced to take abrupt leave from the company and travel overseas to care for him. That left Rohit, Kumar's twenty-two-year-old eldest son, at the helm. Rohit, having returned that very summer to Pune from university in the US, now had to step up run the show in the interim.

When Kumar Gera returned in 1992 after Gera senior's health stabilized, Rohit recalls that seeing the state of the company, his father's first reaction was one of relief, that Rohit had not caused any major problems. Despite some disagreements over construction materials, with Kumar being cost-conscious and Rohit having expensive tastes, the two worked together over the next two decades and learned to complement each other's strengths.

Kumar has tried to trust and understand his children's strengths. When they were teenagers, Kumar had sent his two sons, Rohit and Nikhil, to evaluate a piece of land that Gera was interested in buying. The boys advised against the purchase, citing noise disturbances from trains on the nearby railway track and Kumar had heeded their recommendation.

Of Kumar Gera's three children, Rohit is the eldest. A third-generation real-estate entrepreneur, he is currently MD, Gera Developments. He studied at Doon School in Dehradun and has a double major in building construction and project management, and in economics from the University of Massachusetts. Additionally, he holds an advanced Management degree in Real Estate from Harvard University's Graduate School of Design.

Like his older brother, Nikhil Gera also attended Doon School, later earning a bachelor's degree from the Wharton School of Business at the University of Pennsylvania, and an MBA from the Yale School of Management. Kumar's daughter Rohena, who is in France and is in films, is aware that she can undertake any venture with family support, her funds and her share in the business.

Says Kumar, 'Family businesses have their own challenges among siblings and with elders. I got to understand the importance of the unity of the family when I had certain differences with my father, based on which my brother exited the business. I had that skirmish and realized that this is not good. Luckily for me, my son Nikhil who was at Wharton chatted with famed global family business guru, Prof. John Ward who was taking lectures at Wharton. John gave him a book addressed to me after he chatted. I got into the subject right after that.'

A little later, Prof. Ward came to Delhi for a conference on family businesses, organized by CII. Kumar got his entire family to attend the three-day conference. After that, the Gera family worked seriously to flesh out practices to ensure that family disintegration did not happen. One knotty issue for Kumar Gera—of how to get his second son, Nikhil, involved in the business—was resolved using these learnings. The issue was that having completed higher studies in the US, Nikhil had shifted to India and joined as a director in the company. His wife, an Indian-American and Nikhil's former classmate, did not want to live in India and stayed on in the US. They maintained a long-distance relationship for two years, until Nikhil returned to join her in 2001.

Says Kumar, 'Nikhil was in a dilemma and he eventually chose to return to the US. The group worked around the problem when it decided to start a US operation. This was done with the objective not to expand our footprint overseas but was fundamentally done with the objective of the family staying together.' The Geras also delved deep into the subject of what they are: a family business group? A real estate family? After much deliberation they are now zeroing in on the idea that they are first and foremost entrepreneurs at heart.

Gera Developments is a 100 per cent closely held, family dominated group but with differential shareholding among family members. The plans, challenges, difficulties, legal issues, customer satisfaction, dissatisfaction—nothing is kept to any one individual but discussed threadbare at structured board and family meetings. Today, Kumar has four grandchildren in his growing family.

Having worked with his father closely from 1992 onward, in 1999—after Nikhil's return to India in 1998 post his MBA, and post his joining the Gera group—Rohit took the opportunity to spread his own wings by establishing India Construction, a construction supply dot-com business. This venture differed significantly from his previous experience at Gera, where projects typically took years to complete. At India Construction, Rohit established distribution centres in thirteen cities in under two years, which forced him to learn how to delegate tasks and understand the requirements for rapidly scaling a business. This experience was a new and valuable learning opportunity for him.

With Nikhil's departure for the US in 2001, Rohit returned to Gera. By the end of the 2000s, Gera Development had experienced significant growth. While Kumar gave Rohit the space he needed to expand Gera's design and development capabilities, he also implemented strict fiscal policies to maintain financial discipline within the company. The successful combination of Rohit's ambitious approach to product development and Kumar's conservative financial management allowed Gera to continue operating normally and even grow during the 2008 financial crisis.

In 2011, Kumar transitioned from his role as co-MD to become the chairman of Gera's board of advisors, where he served as a sounding board for the company. This change left Rohit sole MD of Gera. While Kumar focused on developing standard operating procedures, land acquisition, and fostering shareholder cohesion, Rohit focused on professionalizing the company's executive suite.

As for Nikhil, after returning to the US in 2001, he joined the American real estate firm Vornado Realty Trust. He started as a retail associate and worked his way up to become senior vice president for retail and India investments, where he managed Vornado's California retail property portfolio, overseeing leasing, dispositions, acquisitions, development, and property management. He was also responsible for Vornado's India investments. In 2018, Nikhil left Vornado and returned to Gera full-time as ED and president of the company's US operations. While still residing in California, he began using some of the company's capital to build a US portfolio.

As Gera's shareholders were now spread across three continents (Kumar's daughter Rohena being in France), the company's geographic identity was in flux, leading to uncertainties about succession. By 2020, Rohit had been with the company for twenty-seven years and was starting to consider stepping back from day-to-day operations. However, it was not yet clear who would take his place. Rohit's daughter and Kumar's granddaughter, Diya—the oldest member of the family's fourth generation—had been groomed to enter the family business. She had earned her undergraduate degree in Civil Engineering at the University of Warwick and a master's in Real Estate Economics and Finance at the London School of Economics and Political Science. In 2020, when Rohit was thinking of stepping back, Diya, then twenty-five years old, was employed by Deloitte Real Estate in London.

In August of 2020, Diya resigned from Deloitte and returned to Pune where she joined Gera Developments as assistant vice president. In April 2022 she took over as vice president.

Aravind Group: Instilling Family Values and Togetherness

There are many ways in which succession planning is done at Aravind that are deliberate and yet, subtle. So subtle that they are part of the very DNA of the organization.

Today, the Aravind group is over forty-five years old, with the fourth generation being groomed to work in their eye-care hospitals. Even as the youngsters went to school, the entire orientation was how they could and would be part of the hospital conglomerate when they grew up. This way of thinking and living was instilled right from the inception by Dr V.

Says CMO and director, IT & Systems, Dr Kim, 'As we grow up, we are all posted in different hospitals and given some independent charge at a later stage. We are trained to be focused so that we can do our work that much better. This kind of training has been helping us and the thinking also has been helping us to keep our thoughts revolving around the hospital. How can I build more hospitals, how can I add more numbers to reach out and impact that many more people?'

In family businesses, it is generally seen that there is not much pain with regard to intergenerational transition in the first and second generations. The third generation tends to find there is much that is wanting, but the ingrained value framework combined with a bottom-up approach has overcome much of this pain at Aravind.

Says ED Operations, R.D. Thulasiraj, 'The younger generation starts at the bottom. In fact, they get a little more grilling than others. They all have to work in a smaller hospital including a rural posting, which we don't insist for other doctors. For the family members, we say that you have to work for two or three years in a small hospital as a regular medical officer and only then we will allow you to specialize. There is a bit of a disadvantage. But then all of it is grooming them for the long haul. Through generations, as they get into Aravind, they equally appreciate and subscribe to that framework of working which I think is very critical. If the goal is to make money, then Aravind is not the place for them.'

A sense of family togetherness is crucial to ensure that succession planning is successful. At Aravind, cultivating this togetherness takes various forms and shapes. For example, Dr V's sister, Dr G. Natchiar was often the glue in the family. In companies, if the CEO meant chief executive officer, it meant something very different at Aravind: Dr Natchiar was the CEO, the chief emotional officer.

Expert Take by M.S.A. Kumar

At a seminar on 'Future of Family Business' (February 2023) at ISB, Hyderabad, I was fortunate to listen to the Bajaj Group's Sanjiv Bajaj on 'Remembering the legendary Rahul Bajaj'. One episode that Sanjiv narrated stuck with me. As children, Rajiv and Sanjiv used to be fed a gruel made with millets every evening. It seems both used to hate it! One evening, the mother warned the children, 'If you don't drink the gruel, you won't be able to fill your Dad's shoes.' Rahul Bajaj heard this reprimand from the adjacent living room. He went into the dining room and said, much to his wife's dismay, 'even if they consume this nice gruel and get the physical and mental strength, they can't get into my shoes, unless they are otherwise qualified and experienced.' That no helicopter landing is possible was well demonstrated by Rahul Bajaj by nipping aspirations in the bud and pushing meritocracy rather than entitlement.

Professionalization and succession planning are two sides of the same coin. We explained the criticality of professionalization to scale the business as the family-business owner can't do everything by himself. When professionalization is achieved to a great degree to meet short- and long-term goals, and the owner wants to hand over the reins to his NextGen or to a professional from outside the family, the challenge of succession becomes profound.

Let me quote an example here. A thirty-two-year-old son takes over as MD from his father who built the business through a set of dedicated professionals. The father will only play the role of a shareholder as the non-executive chairman of the board.

Within twelve months of the son taking over, two of the senior VPs resign and join the competition. They haven't been able to adjust to the leadership style of the son, which is in contrast to that of the father. The moot point is whether the father failed in preparing the son for the position, or did the senior professionals lack the ability to cope with the different and diametrically opposite leadership style? Either way, the business suffered at least in the short term.

As seen in Sandu Pharma's case, NexGen family members worked outside before joining the family business. This is a good practice to follow along with a good and relevant qualification mandate. It is better if this aspect is notified in the family constitution/charter in the 'entry/exit' section. The advantage of GenNext working in outside organizations is twofold: (i) the youngsters learn how to handle a boss, as they work with experienced professionals. Back home, they learn how to view their father or brother or sister at work as the boss. (ii) It is a good learning for them, as seen in the case of Sandu's fourth generation.

Again, as part of the family constitution, it is better to spell out the succession-planning policy for different senior positions in the organization. Along with the key principles of the policy, the eligibility requirements, the selection process, reporting relationships, onboarding process and mentoring and performance management should be outlined.

7

BEYOND THE FAMILY

Professionalization and Performance Management

As a family business expands and becomes more intricate, there comes a point where it becomes evident that a variety of management skills and abilities beyond that available within the family, are necessary. This is true even when family members possess advanced education. Furthermore, as the business grows larger, family members must transition from primarily operational roles to strategic management roles, while professional managers handle the day-to-day operations. In order for a family business to last multiple generations, professionalization is crucial. However, it is not a natural progression and must be intentionally developed and maintained.

In the early stages of a family business, operations are informal and reliant on trust. However, as the business expands, professional managers are often brought in from outside the family, leading to a separation between ownership and operational control. Trust and loyalty-based systems become less dependable as a result. The company transitions from centralized decision-making and a paternalistic culture to decentralized decision-making and a merit-based culture. This evolution from a simple, entrepreneurial approach to a more complex, professional management style is what professionalization is all about.

While on the subject of meritocracy, as discussed in the previous chapter, owners of family businesses should be conscious of an 'entitlement' mindset. 'Deserve and then desire' is the value that family members seeking to join the business, should follow. Entitlement is confined to ownership, whereas meritocracy dictates management rights. Thus, the need for differentiating ownership and management is a must for a successful family business. Even while inducting family members including GenNext, the tendency of 'helicopter landings' should be avoided. Though family members can have an accelerated career path, it is better to avoid a direct board position at the very outset. This will have two advantages: (i) the new inductee will understand the business processes from the shop-floor level onward, giving them a strong footing in the organization; and (ii) they will have the advantage of working side-by-side with non-family professionals.

Despite the absolute necessity for professionalization as the family business grows, there are many challenges to making it happen well. It is a challenge for family businesses because it is a major transition for both, the business and the family. For the business, it implies transformation from being a personality-driven organization to a process-driven organization. For the family business leader, it involves the process of letting go of managerial control to professional managers.

There are a number of best practices by which family businesses can be professionalized. These include building the right culture for professionals to thrive in, creating mutual trust between professionals and family members, letting go where needed and leaving execution to professionals, establishing performance benchmarks and setting expectations up front and, finally, having a mechanism where emotive and complex issues can be discussed and addressed on an ongoing basis.

Popular Automobiles: Onboarding Professionals

'After my father started the business in 1939,' says MD John K. Paul, 'his four brothers joined the company one by one over a span of ten years. In the initial stages we did have relatives working with us but by the time the second generation, my brother and I, joined, he had decided that relatives were the last people he would have in the company. But whatever help they needed he would provide.'

Today, even though the group has progressed to three generations, there are just five members of the founding family and extended family among its 9,000+ employees. That's a remarkable level of professionalization. It is based on the fundamental belief that the presence of relatives in the company breeds nepotism, which could cleave into the vitals of the firm like termites.

John K. Paul's take on this is, 'Nepotism is not new; it is centuries old. My experience is that if there is a relative in the firm, he slowly starts creating his own circle of employees. Additionally, if you hire one relative then automatically you are open to take more. In the Kuttukaran Popular Group, it is not just about relatives; we have a policy that we cannot take our personal friends into the business, even if they are highly qualified. This is part of our corporate governance policy. We have said no relatives, no friends. Period!'

Towards onboarding thousands of professionals, the promoters' task was made easy by the fact that although 'Popular' is a popular name for many ventures in Kerala, the Kuttukaran Popular Group is among one with the highest brand equity. Over eighty-years-old, it is also one of the oldest private-sector firms in the state. But despite this, while it is not a major task to attract younger professionals, senior officers are not that easy to hire. They are, however, able to hire senior Malayalee professionals who come back to Kerala for personal reasons, like looking after their parents for example.

While hiring and retaining its employees, one of the key messages that the company sends out is that it would like to be benchmarked among the world's most admired organizations. Audacious? The company understands that Popular will not be recognized worldwide, but the messaging is largely for the employees to note that this is the vision, this is the aim. How do they try to do it? By continuously delivering greater value to customers. Being a service organization with about 300 outlets, unlike a manufacturing firm, the points of control are many. At Popular, customer delight has to happen at the point of delivery. One of the key ways this is perfected and done is through a rigorous company-wide training programme. With hundreds of outlets, the only way to make customer service almost perfect and give them a good experience is to empower the employees through a process that the company calls 'by entrepreneurship within'.

Even though the turnover of the group is around Rs 5,000 crore as of date (in 2023), it has hesitated from hiring professionals at exorbitant salaries. Instead, at any given point of time over its decades-long history, Popular has an unwritten policy that it will hire people by what it can afford to pay and not just in relation to what the competition is giving. For some who have an IIT-IIM background, Popular does make some adjustments in compensation though. The company's image, reputation and values have been sufficient so far to attract good professionals. The company has also not insisted on having people only from the automobile industry—it employs people from other domains like retail and consumer goods, as well. The current head of sales came in from a background with past experience in Shell India and Cadbury, and has been with the company for about fifteen years.

But hiring and retaining the top management in particular has still not been easy. For example, one of the CEOs brought in, had an IIT-IIM background and in the five years that he was there brought in a lot of changes. He was then poached at a much higher salary by a Japanese multinational company and it has been a challenge to find a replacement for him.

Onboarding outside professionals and their acculturation is an important aspect. They need to have a fair degree of connection with the family, its values and philosophy. How to replicate the entrepreneurial spirit and the tacit magic of creating value beyond the family, is a challenge for family businesses. Mutual respect between non-family professionals and family members is very important for successful professionalization. Family members may be better at providing outside professionals with effective leadership and guidance, but it is better to leave the execution to the professionals. Emotive and complex issues must be discussed and addressed on an ongoing basis, otherwise, they may become bigger problems in the future. Establishing performance benchmarks and setting expectations upfront, is very important to ensure that the business and family/non-family professionals are able to achieve their potential.

Dodla Dairy: Attracting and Retaining Employees

With about 5,000 employees in all (on its rolls and contractual), Dodla Dairy has a unique culture based on the fact that it is a grassroots organization spread across small villages and districts. Until recently it had a six-day work week. Says Sunil Reddy, 'I will simply say we have more of old-school culture where we look at discipline, being efficient and honest. These are our core values that keep us going. We also assume that people can make mistakes. We understand that our people might not be the smartest of the lot, because we come from an industry that is based in small villages and district headquarters across different regions and states. We get excellent talent that comes in from these Tier II and Tier III cities and towns. They might not be the best speakers of the English language but they are able to communicate with passion and honesty.'

Internal events and group activities are rarely held at five-star hotels. In its earlier days, the organization once held a get together at a lovely five-star hotel, but none of the team liked it. Why? They didn't like to use toilet paper in the washrooms. Many of the employees at this offsite used their hands to eat. Travelling by air on office work was a first for many of them. They preferred to use trains as opposed to planes. But as the company grew, professionals at the senior management level had to step up. Recently Dodla Dairy held an investor meet at a five-star hotel in Mumbai where, even though the senior professionals were not comfortable with the ambience, they put their best foot forward.

Recently, after some good business, Sunil Reddy wanted to open a bottle of champagne. But the CEO looked at the bill and realizing that the bottle cost more than Rs 10,000, wanted to not pop the bubbly. 'We believe that culturally the company has to adapt to the value systems of professionals,' he says. 'That is the main theme of our talent building policy. It is not that we cannot or could not afford. It is just their thought process and what is relevant for them, what is good for them is good for us. That is what I mean by the culture of the company. We sit now on tons of money. But in Dodla, even today, Rs 10,000 is a lot of money.' To date, most senior professionals prefer to fly economy even when they are entitled to business-class travel. However, on Sunil Reddy's insistence, some of them now fly business class on overseas travel.

The younger generation of professionals coming into the company has brought new challenges to maintaining this culture. The NextGen of the promoter family being inducted into the company also want to bring in a more modern and contemporary culture. Slowly, winds of change are coming into the group. But the company believes that this change has to be brought in gradually. Even in this transition and change, authenticity is the guiding light in building the right culture.

While recruiting non-family professionals to scale and grow the organization, reference checks from previous employers will give clues on the cultural fit. There are also psychometric tests available to gauge the candidate's work strengths and environmental fit. The analogy of a liver transplant is relevant in this context. Before the transplant, doctors carry out compatibility tests for the donor and the receiver. Post-transplant the patient is closely monitored on various parameters. All efforts are made to spot and nip problems in the bud, to ensure a healthy environment for the new liver to be accepted. Same is the case when a new professional joins a new organization—the onboarding process has to be planned in detail and problems spotted and nipped in the bud.

We suggest a four-step 'DJID' onboarding process.

Step 1: Demonstrate simple standard operating procedures to the new joinee. This is the 'directing' stage.

Step 2: Jointly carry out tasks along with the joinee through 'coaching' stage.

Step 3: Independent working on specific assignments, wherein the owner of the family business plays a 'supporting' role.

Step 4: 'Delegating' once sufficient trust is developed and the owner is confident the joinee can carry out the tasks with minimum intervention.

We have noticed that when an owner recruits a senior managerial person from a multinational, the tendency to jump to step 4 is common. Independent of the new joinee's past experience and status, it is recommended to go through the four DJID steps. At the same time avoid making the 'halo error'—the tendency of getting a positive impression of a person too soon!

Bhima Jewellers: Establishing Systems and Structures

For the eight-decade old Bhima Jewellers, the journey toward professionalization is a recent phenomenon, just about ten years old. Up to this point, decision-making and daily operations were ad hoc. There was no data to rely on. Most of the top management positions were held by family members, many of whom assumed it was their right to be managing the business.

It was in such circumstances that Bhima Bhattar's son Bindumadhav realized the need for professionalization. He was open to new ideas and that definitely helped. He let go and decided to add new blood and value to the organization. Some of the younger generation of family members also attended conferences and seminars on family business management, especially those hosted by ISB, Hyderabad. This exposure gave them the realization of the hidden potential and opportunity to scale if the group was to professionalize in a big way.

They relied on a bunch of consultants and advisors to introduce the change-management process. Towards this, establishing systems and structures was a key component. The group brought in consultants in the areas of strategy, finance and HR, who helped transform Bhima into a more process-oriented organization. From three professionals at the backend a little more than five years ago, it now has about 120 people including a chief operating officer (COO), a chief financial officer (CFO), chief human resource officer and chief category officer. They first built the mid-level managers and then went on to hire the senior managers. The change in management was not disruptive, but gradual. Simultaneously, the group made sure that the roles of various family members were clear and chalked out.

After having recruited the first few professionals, the family was able to see the change that professionalization could bring. The small changes they saw over the years really convinced them to get very senior people in, who could help increase the bandwidth of the family members and help them let go of a lot of things that they were doing. Says Bindumadhav's son Abhishek, 'Letting go was something that I learnt from my father and I did the same with other senior professionals as well. With this they have freedom to operate and at the same time build in accountability and responsibility. Today, there are performance management systems and governance mechanisms in place, which ensure that everyone is contributing to the organization.'

Being a very old group, Bhima also had a large number of loyalist employees and did not want the new blood to bring insecurity to the older employees.

How did the group overcome these challenges?

There was transparency, communication and objective decision-making based on processes and systems. The group started a performance review system bringing the older employees under this system too. The reviews were not just about individual performance but also what was good for the organization. Additionally, today, the employees themselves have asked for a robust enterprise-resource planning (ERP) system by which they can make faster and better decisions.

The fact that there were outside consultants who were aiding this process also helped. Bhima introduced the process of delegation of authority for the employees, and the 'information, advice, decision and execution' (IADE) approach for the family members prescribed by Prof. Kavil Ramachandran. This approach suggests a clear distinction in terms of just informing after the decision is taken, seeking advice and fully empowered decision-making by the employee. At the board level, there is an audit committee along with an internal audit system. Says Abhishek, 'It has been a smooth transition, not a disruptive one. It was a multi-pronged approach I guess, which helped. It was well thought through.'

Adds Bindumadhav, 'The more we learnt about professionalization we realized how keeping ownership and management separate helps the business grow, and how it can add value to the organization. From Rs 1,200 crore when we started professionalization in 2013, we hope to touch Rs 3,200 crore in 2023. In the end, the numbers also delivered. The conviction started there and we still believe that there is a long way to go in terms of completely professionalizing the company along with the board.'

Towards growth and scaling, the company has moved from a partnership to a private limited company and hopes to take the initial public offering (IPO) route to unlock value and growth.

Challenges in Professionalization

While the above success stories are to be celebrated, the journey of professionalization in family businesses has its fair share of challenges.

While the first-generation members maintain a certain level of unquestioned authority with regard to the professionals, the equation begins to change with the entry of the second generation into the business. Their entry has often resulted in direct conflict with old-timers/loyalist professionals of the previous generation. The patriarch must prepare and sensitize GenNext about the contribution of old-timers to the growth of the business. As the second generation becomes involved in the day-to-day activities of a company, professional managers also want to see greater parity in their roles and performance. The company therefore needs to change its model to one where the family members and professionals work together in an atmosphere of mutual respect.

Professionalization of businesses often fail because the family is not willing to let go their control over the firm. Hence, it becomes key to be ready to let go while transferring control and ensure that the family is mindful of what its own role in the business should be in the future.

Family members have to earn the professionals' respect, even as it has to be given. Mutual trust and respect are fundamental preconditions for any meaningful dialogue or partnership. In family businesses, family members have faster career growth and job security. But job security can become a burden too. Family members are often compared to their predecessors. Those who are not accountable can cause big problems. It also leaves the professional management around them confused. Self-doubt becomes barrier for many younger-generation leaders as they know they are there because of the family and not because of their capability. It is important to listen to professionals. After hiring them, not using their inputs and energies can become a barrier and cause frustration. It is important for the family to speak as one. Educated younger generation leaders who have worked outside and secured skill, can establish credibility and let go of any insecurities or self-doubts.

The roles and responsibilities between the family members and the management must be defined clearly.

Segregation of Roles

SEPERATION OF ROLES BETWEEN FAMILY BUSINESS OWNERS AND PROFESSIONAL MANAGEMENT A MUST

FAMILY BUSINESS OWNERS	PROFESSIONAL MANAGEMENT
• ROCE/capital funding/exit policy/ decision-making process	• Develop and implement strategic business plan
• Risk-identification management	• Business goals, annual business plan, budget monitoring and reviews
• Monitor performance through monthly meetings	• Hire, retain, reward senior executives under CXO level
• Hire, retain and reward CXOs and guide succession	• Groom, monitor, develop successors for key leadership roles
• Groom, monitor, evaluate performance of current and next generation family members	

To facilitate this professionalization process, it can be helpful to establish distinct meetings, agendas, and structures. It is important to prioritize ongoing learning and development, which may involve an assessment centre for both family members and senior executives. Each individual should receive a personalized development plan, with the guidance of mentors and coaches. Effective and compassionate communication is critical, with an emphasis on listening and understanding from both the head and the heart. Clearly defined decision-making processes are also beneficial, with accountability for results and an integration of responsibilities clearly delineated.

The professional inner circle of a family business typically includes individuals who have proven themselves in the industry and have been integrated into the family business. It is important to note that not just anyone can be a part of this group. The CEO or manager of the inner circle must be an advocate for the family and must possess a high degree of credibility within the team. Their background should be impressive enough to gain the trust and support of those family members who are not directly involved in the day-to-day operations. It is critical for the family to make a wise decision when choosing the inner-circle professional at this stage, as selecting the wrong person or someone who is not accepted by other family members could cause significant problems for the organization.

The professional inner-circle of a family business also encounters its own set of distinct challenges. One major obstacle is defining and documenting strategy and policies, which may not be inherently difficult, but can become challenging when attempting to secure cooperation from the family coterie. Family members may not have previously been subject to such scrutiny or required to commit to certain areas, making it difficult for them to buy into the proposed changes. For the professional too, obtaining this buy-in may require a significant amount of effort and time.

The second challenge for the professional inner circle of a family business is to provide a different kind of domain knowledge that may not already exist within the family. It is no longer sufficient to excel in a single area, such as accounting or sales. The professional manager must possess a diverse range of skills and knowledge, including the ability to manage manufacturing and operations, develop brands, and create strategies for developing people. In essence, the professional must wear many hats to succeed in her/his role.

For a family business, it's important to select the most skilled family members to join the business while maintaining a balance between family members and professional managers. This balance should prioritize the organization's best interests and not compromise the values inherent in the family business. If there is alignment between the professional's culture and values and those of the family, professionalizing the business is more likely to succeed. Regardless of the degree of family involvement, maintaining macro-level oversight is crucial.

As families usually hold a significant ownership stake in their companies, they need to step away from their purely managerial perspective and regularly evaluate the company's operations and future plans. It is the board's responsibility to safeguard the interests and value of the shareholders. Given the family's substantial investment in the company, they should participate in the organization's governance by serving on the board and presenting their vision and strategy for the company.

Family businesses that lack structure may find it simpler to give authority to non-family professionals in middle-management positions. However, having a well-defined structure, along with established systems and processes, is crucial to maintain discipline within the organization. Therefore, family leaders must strike a balance that encourages employees to be fully committed to the organization, while also implementing the necessary structure and processes.

Looking Ahead

As family businesses grow and expand, the process of professionalization becomes necessary. However, the factors that influence the behaviours of both family and non-family managers during this transition can be quite complex. The family business leader's willingness to adapt and their ability to effectively manage the challenges that arise during the transition phase, often referred to as the 'No Man's Land,' are the most critical factors in ensuring a successful shift towards professionalization.

In the past, Indian family businesses used to bring in outside managers to professionalize their operations as family members lacked the necessary skills. However, nowadays, family members are often highly educated, blurring the line between professionals in the family and external professionals. As a result, the need for outside professionals has decreased, and family members are increasingly taking on management roles within their own businesses.

Emotional readiness and trust are essential factors that contribute to the success of professionalization efforts in family businesses. However, it is crucial for family firms to understand that solely focusing on personality-driven changes will not lead to long-lasting institutionalization. Instead, a well-defined, documented and clearly communicated process that is followed with discipline and commitment will help achieve wider acceptance and make these changes an integral part of the organization. Changes driven by these institutionalized processes result in a smoother and more sustainable transition of a family business into a fully professionalized organization.

Certainly, it is crucial for the leader to prepare their team to tackle the challenges that come with professionalization. To facilitate this transition, family firms may consider implementing the following measures.

- Clearly defining the roles and responsibilities of both family and non-family managers to minimize managerial ambiguity and reduce potential conflict over areas of control.
- Developing and documenting all business processes and ensuring that they are followed consistently.
- Enlisting the guidance and support of experienced family members, external advisors, independent directors, or senior employees as mentors and advisors to help resolve conflicts and provide clarity in processes, rights, roles and duties of both family and non-family managers.
- Establishing and utilizing structural influences, such as a family council or board, and implementing business decision-making systems and processes to facilitate a smooth transition for both the family and management to a more professionalized work environment.
- Ensuring that professionals and promoters share a common vision and work together to establish governance and secure the company's long-term growth.
- Cultivating a culture of mutual respect, non-threatening communication and providing employees with the freedom to work and enjoy their work.
- Creating a sense of accountability for all individuals, including promoters and professionals.

- To maintain passion and commitment over time, recruiting individuals with integrity and providing them with respect, freedom, and opportunities to take risks. By doing so, employees can grow with the company and contribute to its success.

Expert Take by M.S.A. Kumar

A family business owner's dilemma often is, 'when to professionalize?', especially when he/she feels that 'I can run the business on my own'. Though there is no hard and fast rule regarding the timing, one question assumes significance: 'Can I do it all?'

One can't be an expert in all spheres of management and technology. That realization, along with ambitious scaling-up plans, is the starting point for professionalization. While recruiting a professional, the following questions are relevant. Does the professional:

- have the same values as the family business—value congruence is a must;
- have the capability;
- have fire in the belly; and,
- will she/he fit into the organizational culture? To quote Prof. Peter Drucker, 'Culture eats strategy for breakfast.'
- In the case of large families, the family often grows faster than the business. It will then become challenging to absorb all family members wanting to enter the business. Therefore, it is better to encourage GenNext to choose a career outside

the family following their passion and interest. Absorbing all family members in the business without the required slots can be counterproductive.

Professionalization of a family business is often a loosely used concept. Hidden in this term is the question: 'aren't family members running the business, professionals?'

To be successful and create enduring companies, family members have to work as a team along with professionals.

8

THE POWER OF INTANGIBLE ASSETS

How to Build a Great Brand

THE DICTIONARY MEANING OF THE TERM 'BRAND' refers to a name, term, design, symbol or any other feature that identifies one seller's goods or services as distinct from others. In an interesting aside, there is a little story of how the concept of brand came about.

Centuries ago began the practice of using hot iron to brand cattle to distinguish one's own cattle from another's. In those days, the fields were wide open and there were no fences. Everybody's cattle roamed all over the place. In such a situation, it became imperative to brand one's cattle. Furthermore, those cattle-owners that looked after their cattle better—taking them to the water and to greener pastures to graze—commanded a premium in the cattle markets as their cattle stood out and were easily differentiated from the others. Their brand was sought out by eager buyers.

Ever since, differentiation remains the key regardless of domain.

In the Indian premium hospitality sector, Taj Hotels, the Oberoi group and Evolve Back Resorts each have their own unique position that differentiates each from the others. Similarly, if we turn our attention to great leaders like Mahatma Gandhi, we see that they have their own brand personalities and character. Even among non-celebrities like you and I, each different in what makes us stand out. The moment we talk about a brand, a certain imagery comes to our mind. It is just like a human being.

Why is it important for companies to build strong brands? And how can they do it? One of the fundamental prerequisites for scaling-up and growth is building a strong brand. For example, the Tata group has built a strong intangible asset of ethics and trust in business over more than a century. Similarly, Mahindra and Mahindra in more recent decades has transformed its image from being a conservative family business, to that of a young and dynamic group.

These changes do not happen overnight. They have been deliberately cultivated through investments in marketing and brand-building, as well as internal changes to its culture. Investments in people and organization is also a must in building a brand; the power of intangible assets. Today, the valuation of many erstwhile large business groups pale into nothing when compared to start-ups like Byju's and Zomato, even though many of the start-ups have poor balance sheets in terms of profits and revenues. While there are many ways by which companies can build their brand, we will focus on three important areas.

Evolve Back Resorts: Building a Strong Brand Personality

The Evolve Back group of resorts believes in the power of developing a strong brand personality. In common parlance, the term personality refers to how a person comes across to another and the first impression that he or she makes. How a person looks, how they speak, how well they are turned out and how they carry themselves. In fact, even when you are talking on the phone without seeing the other person, you can still form a strong impression. If the person is courteous your subconscious may register an impression of a nice and pleasant person. Often, employees do not have a second chance to create a first impression. Evolve Back has developed a ten-point blueprint for all its employees.

- **Graciousness.** Derived from the word 'grace', it embodies giving happily to others, so that they feel appreciated and cared for.
- **Cheerfulness.** Evolve Back has an annual prize for the most cheerful employee in a calendar year. The company's leadership encourages employees to be cheerful and smiling at all times.
- **Informally professional.** While most of the employees are not normally required to dress in formal wear, like suits, they nevertheless have to be elegantly dressed. As they say, the first

impression is the best impression. One of the reasons why they are not often in formal wear is because the resort is a leisure brand.

- **Knowledgeable.** Information and knowledge in one's area of work is expected to be above par; as also all basic knowledge about the company.
- **Intelligent.** When placed in a difficult situation, staff members are expected to resolve it as swiftly and in as smooth a manner as possible; i.e., they need to have the smarts to not just resolve the situation, but to do so in an outstanding way.
- **Generosity.** Evolve Back believes it is a generous brand. For example, if a customer calls at the last moment to cancel a booking for a genuine reason, it does cancel the booking with no questions asked and no cancellation fee.
- **Straight from the heart.** Says Jose Ramapuram, 'We want to be known as an organization with employees who smile from the heart. In all our communications, I tell the marketing team especially when you write to a customer or a prospective one across the world that we should always write from the heart and not from the head. It should be emotive writing and communication'; i.e., genuine, not superficial.'
- **Attention to detail.** They say the difference between good and excellent is in the detail. It is very, very important for the employees to be detail-oriented in their jobs. For example, when a communication goes out to guests/clients it is rechecked many times, down to the spelling and grammar, before being sent; at the end of the day a single mistake does not sit well with luxury. Their guests, who are paying such a high price for the product, do not deserve mistakes.

- **Going the extra mile.** How do you delight a customer? To delight a customer, an organization does not have to spend millions of rupees. You just have to go one step beyond his/her expectations. For example, at one of the resorts, a guest found that the water heater was not working. He called the relevant department. When the service person arrived, he not only fixed the fault but also handed over a note of apology from the management along with an anthurium flower. This gesture, beyond the customer's expectation, was much appreciated.
- **Personalized service.** Always a work in progress. The organization is working through data analytics to understand habits and behaviours. For example, to recognize who the guest is by just voice recognition and even knowing whether he or she is left- or right-handed.

Evolve Back's ten-point blueprint is a clear case of building a brand through well-defined norms of employee behaviour. Being in the service industry, the blueprint made a big difference in giving unique and compelling value to their guests.

Evolve Back also believes that its brand architecture is key to the experience the resorts deliver. Beyond this, it also has in recent years focused on creating a brand identity of 'spirit of the land', where every resort reflects the localness of the place in which the resort is located. In 2015, Evolve Back reached out to the Dubai government to set up a new resort there in about 3–4 square kilometres. At the presentation, the Evolve Back team spoke about wanting to showcase the spirit of the Middle East in the architecture, the food and even in staff uniforms. After the presentation, the head of the relevant department got up and stood for about half a minute in silence and then said, 'Fantastic, I am really impressed. I have never seen anything like this. Everybody who makes a presentation to me talks about multi-storey mega steel and glass projects. This is something which is completely new and out of the box.'

That concept of the spirit of the land is also what prompted the group to rename itself from Orange County Resorts to Evolve Back in 2017.

House of Anita Dongre: The CEO as the Brand

Founded in 1995, the House of Anita Dongre is today synonymous with the fashion diva herself. In fact, even though the company was founded by three siblings, they decided to position Anita as the brand ambassador. Along the way Anita, who is the chief creative officer and for all practical purposes the CEO, has become the brand herself. This is another way that a company can build its brand, which in turn can help create an enduring business.

Interestingly, the real persona of Anita is seemingly a paradox. At one level she is associated with high fashion and luxury. At another, she has a simple, down-to-earth personality who is at ease both with global and local people. The Anita Dongre brand captures this dichotomy well and has been assiduously built in this direction.

Anita believes that fashion plays a defining role in enhancing a person's confidence and sense of self. As a brand, the company creates luxurious designs that are versatile enough to transcend places and occasions. Whether it is a bridal lehenga, a sherwani, or a well-cut jacket, the intention is to offer the customer a piece that they will love and wear for many years. There is a lot of ethnic wear in the market but, unlike the group's 'Global Desi' brand launched in 2007, much of it does not combine Indian sensibility with western design.

The Anita Dongre Foundation is also an integral part of the company's brand. Around 2012, the company realized that fashion needed to be sustainable in the true sense, impacting the entire planet and its people. 'Grassroot' was the result of this change in thinking. As mentioned earlier, Anita is an ethical vegan, an environmentalist, a revivalist of local craft and advocates compassionate living, which is why her designs do not use any fur or leather. She shares this worldview with her sister Meena Sehra and brother Mukesh Sawlani, who work alongside her.

Anita Dongre Foundation is a non-profit organization that is committed to making a positive impact on the lives of marginalized communities in India. The foundation's primary focus is on developing livelihood opportunities for women in rural areas by providing them with the necessary skills and training. The Anita Dongre Foundation has given countless rural women a voice and a platform, by providing them with livelihood opportunities and skill training. By doing so, the foundation aims to reverse the trend of job migration and bring employment opportunities back to rural areas in India. The foundation is motivated by a sense of purpose and a desire to make a meaningful contribution to society.

The Anita Dongre Foundation has provided assistance to establish a veterinary clinic in Andheri in Mumbai, in collaboration with the animal welfare NGO, World for All Animal Care and Adoptions. Additionally, the foundation offers support to other NGOs such as Plants and Animals Welfare Society in Thane. Anita Dongre's philosophy centres around creating a better future for both its customers and the environment, by preserving India's cultural crafts and uplifting rural artisans, particularly women. In this way, the foundation strives to act as a catalyst for positive change.

As part of its women's empowerment programme, the Anita Dongre Foundation established Community Tailoring Units in rural areas of Maharashtra, India. Through this initiative, underprivileged tribal women receive professional training in making garments and are offered long-term livelihood opportunities, leading to positive social and economic outcomes. Additionally, the foundation has collaborated with skilled female artisans, who specialize in traditional Indian embroidery.

Anita's personal values of embracing a simpler lifestyle has gradually influenced the company's shift towards an environmentally-friendly and ergonomically-designed workplace that emphasizes conservation. In April 2015, the company relocated its headquarters to a sprawling campus situated amid the lush green hills of Rabale in Navi Mumbai. The property harnesses the power of air, water and sunlight in the most efficient manner possible to establish a work environment that is in harmony with its surroundings. The company is committed to continuously seeking greener alternatives and reducing its environmental impact through conscious efforts. This pursuit of sustainability is an ongoing journey for the company.

Despite the company's strong branding around Anita, the founders are now contemplating the future of the business beyond Anita, considering that the company has been in existence for over twenty-five years and has an over 3,000-strong workforce. To build the institution beyond its founders, the company has brought in a leading private equity firm, General Atlantic, which has made an investment in the first fashion house of its kind in India. This move was partly motivated by the need to plan for the company's future beyond its current leadership. This represents the next phase and challenge for the House of Anita Dongre. Nevertheless, over the years, the company has continued to grow and evolve, embracing change, redefining fashion, setting trends, and making a positive impact on people, animals, and the planet.

ELICO Ltd: Focusing the Brand Around Core Competencies

For ELICO Ltd, the sixty-year-old pioneer in the field of instrumentation design and manufacturing, building its brand was not an easy task. Unlike many of the great brands, which are largely in the consumer facing space, ELICO's clients are largely in the government and industrial instrumentation domains. Says Ramesh Datla, 'We had a clear objective and a view on our brand building very early on. We stressed on the importance of creating and building few core competencies to build a strong brand. If we put our hands into too many areas, we cannot be the masters in any. We therefore decided that our core competencies would be around four pillars.'

Research and development: The first pillar is *research and development* (R&D) where all our R&D work could be patented or copyrighted leading to the creation of a wealth of intangible assets. ELICO's brand equity is strengthened by its R&D, with the motto of Connecting Science and Lab. The company's R&D department has been recognized by the Department of Science and Technology, Government of India as early as 1973.

Partnership: The second pillar is *partnership*. Quite early on in their journey, the management realized that it cannot do all the activities by itself, especially if they are to sustain themselves in the long run. ELICO went about building two sets of interesting partnerships. The first, with CSIR laboratories and University research centres. The academic partnerships are with NIT Warangal, Raichur University and Sri Krishnadevaraya University in Anantpur. The second, surprisingly with some of its competitors. Towards the latter, the company went about building strong IPs with competitor companies. 'An example of our partnerships with competitors is the products we design and manufacture for one of the top analytical instruments company in the world, Thermo Fisher for the last 15 years, which they sell on their brand worldwide,' reveals Ramesh.

Building talent: The third pillar is *talent building*. The interface and the engagements with the universities have helped ELICO in recruiting the right talent. Another aspect of employee pride is that for them, they get good recognition externally when they say that they have worked with ELICO. They are able to display the company's values and ethics wherever they have gone on in their career journey after having worked with the company.

Finally, according to Vanitha Datla, the right talent management helps the company to build employee loyalty as there are a large number of them who have worked multiple decades in the organization. They are one with its culture. She feels that this is an important aspect in brand building and helps in creating a long-sustaining organization.

Building the brand through its association with industry associations, for purposes beyond influencing policy: Finally, the fourth pillar is that of *building the brand*. One way is through bringing indigenous innovative total solutions to the customers and the other is through its association with various industry bodies for various purposes in addition to influencing policy. Both Ramesh and Vanitha Datla have been active in CII for the last 25 years. For example, Ramesh headed various national councils/committees that included IPR Committee, Water Committee, Membership Committee, etc. He has also headed the National MSME Council and has been the State Chairman and the Southern Region Chairman. His role at CII has enabled him to be part of several government committees and also part of B20-G20 held by French Government in 2011 and Mexican Government in 2012, which in turn has helped shore up the brand equity of ELICO.

Focusing on the four pillars of core competencies mentioned above have helped ELICO build its brand, which has been crucial in its efforts to scale growth. Says Vanitha Datla, 'Our focused approach has given us the recognition in the market and in our networks. Today, wherever I go and when I mention the name of ELICO, there is a brand recall from the people that I meet or the fact that they have used our instruments in their academic journey or in their own industries. That recognition also validates the sustainability of the organization. We are happy that our brand gets equated with quality, innovation and trust, because most of our customers have been with us over the last many decades. We have an internal target to retain at least 60 per cent of our existing customers and add 40 per cent new customers every year.'

ELICO is known well in the international markets too, because it is one of the very few, if not the only Indian competition for most of the global players in this domain. The proof of its global renown lies in the many global awards it has won, of which the one from Frost & Sullivan is noteworthy. Their products are also well known through the international exhibitions and conferences that ELICO is part of.

In fact, over the last ten years, at least five global players have approached the management to acquire the company. But, ELICO did not consent. Clearly the company's serious efforts to shore up its brand has certainly helped in scaling the company to greater heights.

Expert Take by M.S.A. Kumar

There is a saying that true family wealth lies not its financial assets but in its human capital. The examples of Evolve Back Resorts, House of Anita Dongre and ELICO emphasize the brand as another family wealth enhancer. Apart from that, a strong brand binds the family together across many generations of the family. Therefore, the issue of sustainability and continuity of the family business beyond three generations can be addressed through the brand to a great extent. GenNext will not do anything that will hurt the family business brand, thereby destroying the institution and the wealth associated.

The contrary is also true. A strong brand alone is not sufficient to keep the business and brand. How many of us remember the iconic vegetable oil brand 'Postman'? Almost 70–75 per cent of Indian kitchens had this brand till 2001, when the brand went bust due to a decades-old feud in the Oomerbhoy family. Millennials and Gen Y will not remember the Postman brand as the last 'D' (destruction) identified by Prof. Kavil Ramachandran, played the spoilsport. This is a good case of even a strong brand not being able to sustain the company!

The values of an organization are defined as the behaviour of employees as practiced over a period of time, encouraged by the organization and that becomes the accepted ways of doing things.

9

LEVERAGING THE EXTERNAL ENVIRONMENT

Influencing Policy-Making for Business and Economic Growth

When the Tenth Five Year Plan was being finalized around 2007–08, Aravind Eye Care, even though it is an individual non-profit organization, had its eyes on the larger national vision of preventing curable blindness. With that in mind, it made a proposal to the Ministry of Health asking that a national five-year budget of Rs 2,000 crore be allotted for eye care. However, the ministry was diffident of taking such a proposal to Yojana Bhavan (the headquarters of the [then] Planning Commission [now Niti Aayog]) as the previous five-year budget was only about Rs 400 crore. Not to be deterred, a team from Aravind led by the redoubtable Dr V, first met (then) Finance Minister P. Chidambaram and then Montek Singh Ahluwalia, who was deputy chairman of the Planning Commission. Though both the finance ministry and the Planning Commission asked for a lot of details, they finally approved a budget of about Rs 1,600 crore. This was a classic case of successful lobbying which, despite being at the macro-level, would have an indirect impact on the growth and scale-up of Aravind Eye Care.

Cut to Kumar Gera and the Promoters and Builders Association (PBA) in the 1990s, which later became the Confederation of Real Estate Builders Association of India. Gera was the president of PBA and realized that there was much that the industry needed in terms of SOPs and support. Fortunately for Gera, Ram Jethmalani became the concerned minister at the Centre. Otherwise, a difficult nut to crack, the minister was like a family member to the Geras. It may have also helped that he was Kumar Gera's neighbour and had bought his father-in-law's apartment in Pune.

On a relaxed afternoon at the Delhi office of the minister, along with a group of six colleagues, the CREDAI made a detailed presentation on the acute imperative for repealing the Urban Land Ceiling Act. Says Gera, 'We were able to talk to him, explain the realities of the writing on the wall; that it would be the death knell of real estate development. We also explained why the Act was bad for the economy and the nation. He understood the importance and really took it upon himself and finally the Act was repealed. It was during a period when real estate development was very patchy in the country. It was not at the pace and growth at which you see today. I attribute a key reason for the growth of the sector to the repeal of the Urban Land Ceiling Act.'

Sanjaya Mariwala founded the Association of Herbal and Nutraceutical Manufacturers of India (AHNMI) with the purpose of policy advocacy for the nutraceutical industry. Says Sanjaya, 'I work with industry players and policy-makers in shaping the course of the industry in order to position the Indian Nutraceuticals Industry as a global leader.' This move from Sanjaya will surely benefit his company Omni Active Health Technologies.

Influencing Policy-Making

Successful entrepreneurs leverage the external environment for personal, business and economic growth. In some ways, all three are intertwined. One of the most common ways to achieve the above has been the membership and leadership of apex industry associations like the CII, the Federation of Indian Chambers of Commerce and Industry (FICCI) and the Associated Chambers of Commerce and Industry (ASSOCHAM). Business leaders like Rahul Bajaj, Anand Mahindra and M.V. Subbiah, while closely involved in the leadership of the above industry organizations, have derived personal and professional clout, which have in turn helped their businesses.

Says Sanjaya Mariwala, 'The advantage of being with industry associations is that you get close proximity with the government. The government learns to appreciate who you are and you learn to appreciate what the government does and why it does what it does, the way it does it. I think these are significant advantages of being active participants of associations and leaderships. I got involved with CII and taking up leadership there I think gave me further confidence in leading my own company.'

Mariwala also believes that apart from helping to manage the company's external environment, memberships like that of CII also help in personal and professional development. 'You learn a lot when interacting with other people with similar style, stature and profession. You also interact with professionals and interact with other family members who are owners of businesses as well as senior managers of businesses. You learn a lot from them. You can also transfer a lot to them in terms of your own learning. There is a two-way exchange that significantly helps.'

Aravind Eye Care feels that an abiding lesson at the advocacy level is that influencing macro level policymaking helps the sector grow and the institution scale-up indirectly. It also believes that one is able to influence the bureaucracy when hard evidence is presented to them.

But even then, it was still not part of the government policy. Aravind did a population-based study that looked at the outcome of people who had been operated for cataract. The high-powered thick soda-bottle glass lenses that were in use post cataract surgery during our grandfathers' generation, were replaced with the new intraocular lens. Prior to the intraocular lens, an Aravind study found that over 40 per cent of the people who had undergone the traditional cataract surgery continued to be blind, largely due to lack of access to the high-powered glasses to help them see.

Aravind's ED operations, R.D. Thulasiraj, presented all these data to then health secretary Dr Sujatha Rao. 'She got really upset,' he recalls. 'She said we really have to change this. Then policies came in; every district had a microscope, districts had supply of intraocular lenses, surgeons were trained and lot of things happened. With the result the country's cataract surgeries went up from about a million surgeries to about five million surgeries within a decade. We can't totally claim credit for doing this. What I am saying is that these kind of approaches and advocacy are able to bring about change at scale.'

If we move away from eye care and health sector to the dairy sector, it is another unique example of how, in the traditionally dominant cooperative dairy segment, the private sector has been able to make strong inroads. Some of this has been achieved through strong lobbying.

The work of Dr Verghese Kurien in shaping the cooperative movement in the country has been pioneering. It helped the farmers at a particular point of time and also helped develop Amul and the National Dairy Development Board (NDDB).

The dairy sector was opened up to the private sector in 1995 under the Narasimha Rao government at the Centre, under a provision called the 'Milk and Milk Products Order'. Over a quarter of a century later, a recent CRISIL report states that the share of the private sector and that of the cooperatives is almost equal. Says Sunil Dodla, 'At a point of time when there was no money in the system, the government had interfered, like in aviation, and the dairy sector was a part of that exercise. Today, we are fighting for the same cause. The cooperative idealism of early days is dying. In cooperatives, they call the farmers their shareholders. And for us, the farmers are our as stakeholders. We have worked hard to bring about a change in the perspective of the government and the landscape.'

Sunil Dodla says that one of the key insights from the development of the dairy private sector in India is that government intervention is still vital to creating the necessary conditions for private enterprises to thrive, and it can be highly effective when planned with a long-term, full-system approach. The private sector needs a level-playing field and the work of Dodla and others through the dairy industry association has partially been responsible for a change in the government's approach, in this direction.

Being part of CII and having held leadership positions in the industry association has helped Ramesh and Vanitha Datla of ELICO. When Ramesh was the chairman of CII's national committee on intellectual property, ELICO signed a memorandum of understanding with NIT, Warangal at a CII seminar on higher education. Most of the Indian clients of ELICO are from the government or public sectors and academia. Similarly, when Vanitha was the Telangana chairperson of CII, it helped the company directly and indirectly in forging links with its clients and scaling up the business.

Says Vanitha, 'The networking opportunities have really helped us. I think I was able to bring a lot more visibility into the industry circles about our product and our services. While ELICO is a very well-respected and well-known brand, somehow within the local industry I felt, especially with the government, that they were not understanding in which areas we were actually present in and how our R&D value was being able to bring solutions to certain sectors like water and soil.'

Adds Vanitha, 'I remember when I had taken over as CII chairperson and we were meeting up with a lot of government leaders, at every presentation I was able to bring out our latest solutions, especially the soil and agriculture departments. That evinced a lot of interest among senior people in the government. We were able to get invitations to a lot of states where we made presentations and that in turn helped sustain our business.'

Many of the leaders of leading national companies, like Uday Kotak of Kotak Mahindra, started at the lower levels of industry associations and rose up to become the president of an organization like CII. It is a gradual process but one that is worth investing in. One needs to have the vision, ambition and some money to invest in these opportunities.

Beyond the industry associations, there are many other platforms like the Young President's Organization (YPO), The Indus Entrepreneurs (TiE) and the Family Business Network (FBN) that promote personal and professional development. For example, all of the above are global organizations which have country and regional chapters. Being part of them helps one inculcate a world view.

Leadership positions in them also helps business leaders to develop their own personal leadership styles and abilities. For example, Vanitha's leadership position in the Indian Women's Network of CII has also helped her build professional relationships with women leaders of India Inc. Similarly, FICCI has the much-developed FICCI Ladies Organization (FLO) which does some yeoman work in the area of women leadership at both state and national levels.

Expert Take by M.S.A. Kumar

I have seen that the vision and perspective that comes from networking is different (from that which one can normally acquire), and helps those family business owners who are well networked and part of industry associations in scaling their business. As seen in many examples quoted earlier, leveraging the external environment can be a route to scaling the business. I have also seen in this regard that many family MSMEs, especially those that are at the regional level, do not recognize the power of networking and its potential to help build businesses.

The YPO is a global leadership community of extraordinary young chief executives. A GenNext member of the family of one of my business clients is an active participant in the YPO Forum—a group of eight to ten YPO members who meet on a regular basis to explore challenges in a confidential environment. When he aired some challenges he was facing in his family business, another YPO forum member suggested he contact me; that forum member was my client. Again, the power of networking.

John Paul of Popular Automobiles got the idea of having a constitution from the Family Business Summit organized by the Malayalam business magazine *Dhanam*. Prof Kavil Ramachandran was a speaker at the seminar. Again, another positive outcome from networking!

Networking is also useful for answering the critical question in succession planning: 'What next?'. To quote B.V. Mohan Reddy, chairman of Cyient, 'While handing over the reins of Cyient to Krishna, my son, I came into philanthropy, NASSCOM and in

CII Southern Region. This indirectly helped in me not meddling with Cyient after Krishna took over as the Managing Director.' Many family business patriarchs find it difficult to hand over the reins to a professional CEO/GenNext, in the absence of alternate activities. In some cases, I have also seen the idling patriarch suffering deterioration in physical and mental health!

10

NEXT FRONTIER

Going Global

INDIAN COMPANIES GOING GLOBAL IS NOT A NEW phenomenon. In fact, over the years, there have been three distinct waves in this direction. In the 1970s and 1980s, a few business groups like that of Aditya Birla, the Lohias and L.N. Mittal (father of Lakshmi Mittal of Arcelor Mittal) set foot overseas, particularly in Southeast Asia. The second wave was in the latter half of 1990s after India's economic liberalization, when the country's foreign exchange reserves became better and the government liberalized rules for overseas investment. During this phase, the Tatas, Mahindras and the Godrej family too aggressively acquired overseas companies. Finally, in the 2000s, technology-driven companies like Infosys, Wipro and NIIT expanded both into the western and eastern markets.

Additionally, in the past decade, there has been a significant shift in overseas investment destinations (OIDs). In the first half, overseas investments were focused on resource-rich nations like Australia, the UAE, and Sudan. In the latter half, overseas investments were directed toward nations offering greater tax advantages, such as Mauritius, Singapore, the British Virgin Islands, and the Netherlands.

The above successes happened despite the slowdown of the global economy due to Covid-19. Government policies and reforms helped in boosting overseas direct investment (ODI). For example, the government reduced restrictions on Indian companies investing overseas by removing the cap on raising funding through the pledge of shares, local assets and foreign assets. Finally, India has been instrumental in signing various memoranda of understanding (MOUs) and free trade agreements (FTAs).

While the above is largely applicable to large business houses, the presence of medium-scale family businesses was virtually nil till the early 2000s. But since then, a small group of lesser-known family businesses have established strong business ties with foreign shores. We profile strategies of five such firms: Bhima Jewellers, Dodla Dairy, House of Anita Dongre, Sandu Pharmaceuticals and Aravind Eye Care.

Sandu Pharmaceuticals: Thrust on Exports

Former prime minister of Mauritius, Anerood Jugnauth, who passed away in 2021, was an ardent fan of the products of Sandu Pharmaceuticals. The company regularly sent its product range to him. A few years ago, on an official visit to India, he had taken special interest to come down all the way from Delhi to Sandu's factory in Goa to inaugurate a herbarium. He also discussed the possibility of setting up an ayurveda products factory in Mauritius.

Mauritius is one of the eighteen countries that Sandu Pharma exports its products to. The company started in a modest way, exporting first to neighbouring countries in South Asia like Nepal, Sri Lanka and Bangladesh. It then expanded to other countries in the region such as Singapore and Mauritius and then to East and West Africa to countries like Kenya, Ghana, Botswana and Nigeria. Later, it pitched its tent in the Latin American nations of Guatemala, Costa Rica and Bolivia. Russia and Central Asian countries like Ukraine were also part of Sandu's orbit. In fact, despite the ongoing war between Russia and Ukraine, orders are pouring in to Sandu from both countries. It has also reached the shores of Europe primarily exporting to the Netherlands, Germany and the UK, and now also to the US.

Sandu was able to succeed in export markets because it had an understanding of how to deal with markets in non-local regions (i.e., outside of its founding home-base Maharashtra) from very early on. In the late 1800s and early 1900s, many of the raw materials used in the ayurveda products came from the regions that are now in Afghanistan and Pakistan. Raw materials for Sandu products like saffron and pomegranate used to be brought on behalf of the suppliers by Kabuli Pathans who rode down to Amritsar on horseback to before gradually moving further in to North India and then southwest to Maharashtra.

While the Pathan carriers came throughout the year, the actual-owner suppliers came only once a year. They used to send a message before they came and the money had to be kept ready in sacks. They never counted the money. But if it was not paid on time, the credit-worthiness of the buyers would come down. Non-executive director Shashank Sandu says these early cross-border transactions helped the company greatly to understand global market methods when it started and later developed exports.

In recent years, two broad developments have helped in the exports of ayurveda products from Sandu. The first is the growing presence of exports through the e-commerce route, especially in the post-Covid years. The second is the setting up of the Ministry of AYUSH by the Narendra Modi-led government.

Dodla Dairy: Choosing the Right Markets

For Sunil Dodla Reddy of Dodla Dairy, global conquests are an integral part of its growth strategy. But he is prudent enough to realize that this approach has to be tailored to the skill sets that Dodla Dairy has.

Dodla Dairy's modest presence in East Africa is driven by the synergy between the skill sets of Dodla Dairy' people and the cultural ethos of East Africa. For example, the experience of procurement, processing and distribution along with lower overheads have helped Dodla to integrate better in the East African businesses. Says Sunil Dodla Reddy, 'Perhaps, we won't be able to integrate that much into French Africa because the language there is a problem. Now that we have entered Africa, it gives us a little more confidence to move further globally.'

The company has also set up a company in Singapore. Southeast Asia, again, gives Dodla the advantage of cultural affinity. However, Dodla is slow in moving into the US and European markets because the margins are lower there and the operating systems are different. Sunil Reddy, however, adds that, 'We will get there one day. For now, we are learning to go wherever we have strengths.'

Globally, the dairy market is dominated by European, Pacific and US companies like Nestlé, Lactalis, Danone, Kraft Heinz and Fonterra. Many of them are very old and established firms, between seventy to a hundred-years-old. Interestingly, the older firms among the above, like Fonterra of New Zealand, are cooperatives (much like our Amul), while the relatively newer Western dairy companies are from the private sector.

Like many of the above companies, which started as dairy firms selling milk, cheese and butter and slowly moved up the value chain to become wholesome food companies, Dodla also plans to do the same in India and overseas.

Competing globally against the established firms will not be easy but is something that Dodla will have to do in a medium-term horizon. For the present, it will have to consolidate and expand further in India. Says Sunil Dodla Reddy, 'There is so much to do. The canvas is so large and so vast. We had a good opportunity to start with a good base. From there we have branched off into multiple opportunities that we got, especially overseas. Our long-term brand proposition is to give good nutrition to people. That is our canvas to play for the next twenty-five years.'

House of Anita Dongre: Building a Global Brand

With an existing global brand equity on the back of high-profile clients like Kate Middleton, Hillary Clinton and Priyanka Chopra, setting up an Anita Dongre flagship store in upmarket Manhattan, SOHO was a natural extension. In 2018, when the 4,000 square feet store was opened, it was perhaps one of the first Indian retail fashion stores in the US. Some of the lesser-known Indian fashion brands had set up stores in areas like New Jersey where there is a heavy concentration of middle-class Indian consumers. By setting up the store in high street New York, the Anita Dongre group wanted to target the rich Indian and South Asian clientele apart from some of the exclusive American clients. Traditionally, the high-networth Indian-Americans used to fly down to Mumbai or Delhi when they had to buy occasion wears for weddings and other family functions. Now, it was available in the US itself. In the US, it tasted early success with its occasion and bridal wear because the Indian diaspora is really huge and very powerful. Yash says that their per capita and other disposable incomes are on the higher side compared to a lot of other expat communities. But even though the House of Anita Dongre does modern international style clothing, it is true to Indianness in terms of design and aesthetics. Even for the American market, it works only with Indian craftsmen.

Says Yash Dongre, business head, House of Anita Dongre, 'When we set up our store in New York we had customers landing up from day one. Many of them even felt emotional and some would even tear up saying that there were so proud to see an Indian brand making it big globally.'

Expanding overseas, the next destination after New York was Dubai, where it opened another flagship store in the high-end Dubai Mall in 2023. Counterintuitively, even though the United Arab Emirates (UAE) has a large Indian population, here the business model is different. About 75 per cent of the customers are Arab and international ones and the rest are Indians. Additionally, Dubai Mall is very selective about the kind of brands they partner with. Normally, a brand would get preference at the mall after the presence of about two to three stores in Dubai. But because, the Anita Dongre brand had a high global brand equity, it got selected with the first store itself. This strategy also speaks volumes about the changing nature of Dubai in recent years. Moving forward, within the region, the company plans to expand within Dubai and in other parts of UAE and the Middle East. Further, the group is planning more stores in the United States, other parts of North America and the United Kingdom.

Yash says that a few factors have contributed to its success in going global. To start with, the first-mover advantage of an Indian fashion retail in that market. Second, it has customized and adapted its positioning and brand strategy from market to market. Third, listening to what the consumer wants. In the last three years, it has done a lot of market research in the UAE region and did a couple of exhibitions, which gave the company a lot of learnings that were used to create products to that market. For example, the company is mulling over introducing an existing brand of theirs called Global Desi, which is in the

Indo-fusion category. It has also created local websites where the US and Dubai have own websites apart from the main corporate website. Finally, close monitoring and being close to the market is important. For example, initially when it was setting up the US presence, Yash was based there. Now, that it is focusing on the Dubai market, Yash has shifted his base to Dubai.

Aravind Eye Care System: Global Partnerships

The Aravind Eye Care System has a training and consulting arm called Lions Aravind Institute of Community Ophthalmology (LAICO). This arm is responsible for training and consultation services to enhance eye care in other eye hospitals across the developing world. The Aravind Eye Care System is known for its innovative approach to eye-care delivery and is considered a model for other developing countries.

The work of LAICO has had a significant impact on eye-care programmes globally. Its focus on consultancy, capacity building, management training, and research has helped to improve eye-care delivery systems in developing countries. By collaborating with over 370 hospitals in India and 30 other developing countries and training over 3,463 professionals from 84 countries, LAICO has contributed to an estimated additional 8,00,000 surgeries annually.

Aravind engages in partnerships when there is a strong alignment of values. An example of this is its partnership with Muhammad Yunus, the Nobel Laureate and founder of Grameen Bank in Bangladesh, to set up a network of eye hospitals. As part of the partnership, doctors and young rural girls recruited from Bangladesh underwent a year-long training programme at Aravind. The success of this initiative was greatly influenced by the strong brand reputation of Grameen Bank.

Carlos Orellana from El Salvador and Jhavier Okhyusen from Mexico were collaborating on a project in Madrid in 2005 when they stumbled upon the best-selling book *The Fortune at the Bottom of the Pyramid*, by C.K. Prahalad.[1] They were particularly drawn to the section on Aravind. Five years later, they were motivated to establish an eye centre in Mexico after attending a workshop on eye-care management offered by LAICO. They pooled together their savings for this project, marking the Aravind model's first foray into Latin America.

During the early 1990s Dr Geoff Tabin, who has scaled all seven of tallest mountains in the world, and Dr Sanduk Ruit, a young doctor from Nepal, established a centre in Nepal that focused on high-volume, high-quality eye care. Their inspiration for this project came from Aravind and its successful model. They travelled to rural areas to perform cataract surgeries and established a training centre and skill-transfer programmes in Nepal and sub-Saharan countries.

The Aravind model has served as an inspiration for the establishment of some centres in the US in recent years too.

Bhima Jewellers: Creating a Start-Up Overseas

Have you heard of a family business group that partitioned itself several decades ago only to come together again more recently, when an opportunity for growth presented itself through going global? Think Bhima Jewellers.

In 2014, the ambitious yet onerous task of taking Bhima Jewellers global with its first store and presence outside India in Dubai fell on twenty-five-year-old Abhishek, the dynamic grandson of the founder Bhima Bhattar and son of B. Bindumadhav. It was not easy because it meant taking along his uncles and cousins who often were not on the same page. But the effort was all worth it.

The rationale for Dubai was an easy decision. With around five million non-resident Indians (NRIs) in the Middle East, which accounts for about 30 per cent of the total NRIs in the world, it is a natural first-stop for any company wanting to target this consumer group. Of this number, around 3.8 million are from Kerala. Furthermore, Dubai is often considered the alternative gold capital of the world after Kerala.

Says Abhishek, 'It was like any other new venture and we did have the brand recognition by the Indian diaspora there, especially the South Indian communities. This was a business that my father and my uncles asked me to kind of set up and manage. So, it was like a real entrepreneurial experience for me. It took me out of my comfort zone and today I am what I am because of those Dubai experiences.'

The new geography came with its attendant challenges: new customers, shifting the initial team from Kerala, setting up banking facilities and getting the funds for operations from Kerala, which had its regulatory issues, setting up the right security infrastructure, getting the jewellery made in Kerala and importing it into UAE. Along the way, Bhima also re-learnt the super important fact that location is a priority in a market like Middle East, which has a fast life. In fact, it had to move out of one location and set up a new one when it was realized that the first one was not at the most appropriate place.

Clearly, the journey was not easy. As the saying goes, sales are vanity, profit is sanity and cash flow is reality. Bhima in the Middle East was not able to generate profits for many years after it started. The partners in the business—the extended family members who had come together for this venture—started to get edgy as to how long they would have to keep investing before they could generate profits and reinvest that.

Looking back, Abhishek recalls, 'I did not see the initial failure as one. By nature, I am very optimistic and hopeful. We were burning cash initially and I did give a commitment over and over again that the business would turn around. I think that was the biggest challenge. The partners only had half that confidence but the biggest motivation for me was to make them believe in the future of the project. In fact, just about three years back, one of the partners even went to the extent of saying that we should just wind up the global operation. I said, hold on. If you want to exit you can, but I am sticking around here. The conviction, hard work, patience and the passion paid off. We have started generating operating profits since 2020. Now I think there is no going back.'

Despite these hurdles, there were a few critical elements that helped Bhima in cracking the Dubai market: (i) it retained some of the traditional aspects that its products are famous for, like antique and temple designs with some degree of tweaking. (ii) Unlike in India, where stand-alone stores are in vogue, in Dubai Bhima went in with the local trend of having stores in the large format malls. (iii) With Dubai being a global megapolis, Bhima targeted the contemporary, ultra-modern woman even within the NRI community.

The Covid years of 2020 and 2021 also hit the company hard, especially in a new market when there was already ambiguity as to how things would pan out. Competition existed, but overall, the group focused on three dimensions: location, products, team and consistency. They believed that if they kept their vision and execution simple, worked hard and stayed consistent, it would pay off one day.

Now that they know what works and what does not, they are expanding and opening new stores. Furthermore, having overcome the initial challenges and Bhima making an impact on the Dubai market, they now believe that they have got the right learnings and business model for further global expansion and growth. Other than the remaining emirates, the company is also looking towards the UK, US, Singapore, Malaysia and Australia, studying these areas for possible opportunities and expansion. These are also regions with concentration of the Indian community, though unlike the Gulf, the majority are not Keralites.

There are a number of lessons from Bhima's global foray for other family MSMEs who want to go global as a means of scaling-up. First, Bhima did not go for an all-out high-investment strategy. It used the Middle East—a region with a high NRI population—as a test case, taking relatively limited risks. In this way, the company was able to build upon the brand equity that it had into a focused, legacy brand. Bhima sent a member of the younger generation, Abhishek, as the leader of this project, who perhaps had a lot more passion and energy to last out the gruelling early difficult years.

Expert Take by M.S.A. Kumar

The biggest challenge for MSMEs, family managed or otherwise, is understanding the culture of the target countries for going global. While I was heading AVT Natural Products, the board decided to set up a subsidiary in China to grow marigolds; marigold extract is used for poultry pigmentation (xanthophyll) and eye health (lutein for prevention of age-related macular degeneration [AMD]) in the global market. We achieved success and during one of my visits, I called the factory head and congratulated him on the excellent performance. The local CEO was Chinese and he told me the same evening, 'You have put me in a challenging situation as the factory manager will now ask for a special bonus.' While I was looking for a Chinese JV partner for the company, one of the potential candidates mentioned, 'if there is no profit in any transaction, we won't honour the contract. That's how we do business in China'. We then decided to go for a 100 per cent own subsidiary with a Chinese CEO! When going global a calibrated location-by-location approach is suggested, giving the owners a chance to learn from mistakes and correct them as they go along.

Going global, apart from scaling, helps in risk-mitigation as well. The challenges of going global sometimes brings the family together, as seen in the case of the separated siblings and cousins in the case of Bhima. Scaling through going global also helps family businesses open the door of the large international markets as well as sourcing raw materials. Sandu Pharma found that it gained a sourcing advantage as it went global, as did AV Thomas & Co., Chennai.

AV Thomas & Co. used to export raw spices to the global market. One of its customers was McCormick & Co., USA, the global number one spice company. It so happened that finally McCormick decided to set up a 50:50 joint venture with AV Thomas for processing value-added spices: AVT McCormick Ingredients Pvt Ltd.

11

UNLOCKING VALUE AND WEALTH

Exit and Reinvest and Infusion of Private Equity

FAMILY BUSINESSES ARE INCREASINGLY LOOKING TO unlock value and wealth for a variety of reasons. Traditionally, many of them raised capital through debt from banks as they did not want to reduce the family ownership control and management.

Capital is a critical requirement to grow a business. Says private equity investor and partner and co-founder, Amicus Capital Partners, T.V. Sunil, 'Because the country is growing, if you want to create value, you need to grow along with the country or faster than the country's growth. Otherwise, you will only be losing value. More and more new ideas are coming up every day. Today, fortunately, capital is available at stages of growth of a company. That is the big difference as compared to the past.'

Group Meeran: Exiting and Reinvesting

After Senior Meeran passed away in 2011, Navas and Firoz scaled Eastern. Navas took over the reins of the company with Firoz to assist him. Two years later Firoz became the MD and Navas assumed the role of chairman and moved out of managing the day-to-day operations of the company. He wanted Firoz to have independent charge of running the company. The Orkla merger was accomplished by the joint efforts of both.

Over the years the brothers realized that with the strong establishment of systems and processes, scaling challenges had diminished substantially. With that, they were also able to spend some of their time outside Eastern Condiments on their other investments like Sunidra Mattresses and Eastern Treads. A newer venture, Eastea was becoming a success and they realized that it was just their cup of tea. The third generation and the better halves of the Meeran brothers were slowly blossoming and moving into the operations of Group Meeran.

Although both Navas and Firoz are relatively young, 54 and 40, respectively, they look back with gratitude at what God has bestowed them with, and feel they would like to give back to society and the nation. Specifically, they would like to nurture entrepreneurship at scale outside Eastern and hope to impact a large number of youth in particular.

Eastern is perhaps one of the first family businesses in Kerala to have professionalized itself. Following this, the Meeran brothers started looking at ways of how they could gradually exit Eastern Condiments and unlock wealth and value. Consistent growth, efficient workforce, a good value system, robust future prospects, strong visibility and brand recall enabled Eastern to obtain a good valuation for the acquisition by Norway's Orkla ASA, in a deal implemented through its Indian subsidiary MTR Foods in 2020. The deal valued Eastern at Rs 2,000 crore, an enviable accomplishment hitherto unheard of in the corporate history of Kerala.

Together, MTR and Eastern can come out with a bouquet of products to tempt any refined palate. Apart from the equity that Orkla has brought in, Eastern has benefited through multiple learnings, prominent among them being board management and new standard operating procedures. This partnership has helped professionalize Eastern and make it world-class. An important reason why this partnership has been successful is that Eastern and MTR are run as two full-fledged entities rather than being merged into one; Orkla's global game is to be fully local. There are many knowns and unknowns and having the flexibility to work through two successful brands is very useful.

Every organization is driven by how it designs the future. What has brought Eastern to this point may not take it to the next level. Group Meeran now wants to support the younger entrepreneurs who have great ideas, mentor them, these are things that the company's future will contain.

OmniActive: Infusion of Private Equity

Leading global growth private equity firm, the US-based TA Associates, acquired a significant stake in 2021 in OmniActive

Health Technologies, which offers a wide range of premium, scientifically-validated, natural nutraceutical ingredients. Founder and Executive Chairman Sanjaya Mariwala has further increased his personal holding.

Established in 2005, OmniActive seeks to improve lives by enhancing nutrition and wellness through science and innovation. A leader in health solutions, the company offers a range of premium natural ingredients that are innovative and scientifically-validated for dietary supplementation and nutritional fortification. OmniActive works with leading human nutrition brands and manufacturers across the world to improve the health and well-being of consumers through a solution-oriented approach. The company has R&D and manufacturing operations in Pune, Hosur and Thane in India; and sales and distribution operations in India, the US, Europe, Asia, Australia and Latin America.

Sanjay Mariwala states that this partnership, 'has significantly helped us in doing three things. One is it helped us look at international benchmarking with other companies as well. We further improved our margin and profitability. Second, we have been able to bring in some new members to the team. We have been able to recruit better. The third thing they are helping us do now, is to look at an international acquisition.'

The whole objective of bringing in a professional team is to start scaling much bigger heights. It will continue on its chosen three-pronged path: (i) to continue to innovate and create new products; (ii) to grow its existing products in existing markets. Today, it has product leadership positions in the US market. (iii) It now needs to establish this leadership in Europe and Asia as well. It could also grow through acquisitions to bring to market new products and new teams.

There are companies that are reluctant to bring in private equity because of the scrutiny that it brings on board. To them Sanjaya Mariwala has this to say, 'You know whether you are clean or not. Nobody else knows that. You have to mentally make up your mind to say we have to move the clean way. Then you have to go and take away the bad practices of taking cash out of the company, writing family bills into the company … these governance issues are to be dealt with. Raise your salaries. Increase your compensation for the management team. Pay them well and then be able to bring board members also into the company. We continue to make some of those changes in the process. And that has made such a big difference to the board as well. I think governance is the most important criteria that one needs to be thoughtful about, when we bring in private equity. And that dialogue has to be had in very clear terms. You can't bring in private equity and then think of what changes you need. You need to make the changes and then bring in the private equity.'

Expert Take by M.S.A. Kumar

Diluting ownership and an outsider sitting on the board is always an emotional decision and a headache for the family business owner. What I found is that the new generation in most cases is okay with it, but it remains a no go for the family patriarch. The case studies of Eastern, IBS, and Eastern clearly establish the 'vision–action connection: jaise lakshya, vaise karma' (discussed in Chapter 4). If the family board has the vision of scaling up and taking care of the career ambitions of GenNext, that becomes the lakshya or goal. Then of course, the karma or action follows.

Like Sanjaya Mariwala of OmniActive stated, the first step is to run a clean show; clean accounts adhering to the highest standards of governance are a prerequisite. Navas Meeran of Eastern started the process of unlocking value by roping in Deloitte as the auditor before getting the private equity on board. The chairman and board should prepare the organization to accept the new shareholders. Apart from clean accounts, professionalization therefore is a key element in the level of preparedness.

Let me narrate a boardroom experience here as an independent director. The MD of a private equity company asked the chairman (who was the founder and 60 per cent shareholder) why the company had a guest house in Delhi. It was of course for company's senior executives to stay in during visits, but its major occupancy showed visits by the chairman's friends and relatives. A very delicate and sensitive question and subsequent discussion at the board.

There is also this mistaken notion that PE brings funds for scaling-up. While funding is one of the key objectives, there are many other benefits: (i) sharing of best industry practices with PE exposure to similar industries; (ii) setting up robust governance systems as good PEs slowly nudge the company to IPO readiness; and (iii) driving effective performance management systems.

12

WHAT NOT TO DO

Learnings from Mistakes

'LEARN FROM THE MISTAKES OF OTHERS. YOU CAN'T live long enough to make them all yourself,' said Eleanor Roosevelt. 'Everyone makes mistakes.'

What not to do is more important than what to do!

From the twelve successful family businesses case studies narrated in previous chapters, we have gained a deeper insight into processes, approaches and even some mistakes committed by them. And in this chapter we will explore some of these mistakes. In some cases, but not all, we will not be mentioning the names of family businesses as they would like to keep their identity confidential.

Diversification

Many family businesses venture into unrelated diversifications. While diversification is a proven route to scaling and growing the business, going to entirely an new vertical unrelated to the core needs to be thought through. During early days at Eastern, Navas Meeran ventured into supply of tread rubber and other materials by incorporating Eastern Treads Ltd in 1993. 'We assumed that we could easily replicate the success of spices and condiments in the retreaded tyre business,' he says. 'It turned out to be a steep learning curve at a time when the group was resource-strapped.'

For scaling and growth of business, two strategic options are always available—stick to the knitting or diversify. While diversifying to unrelated verticals, the owner of a family business should do a 'capability, return, risk and potential' study. Managerial manpower bandwidth is critical for scaling and more, if it is an unrelated diversification.

Halo Error

One medium sized FMCG company hired an experienced sales and marketing head from Hindustan Lever as the CEO. Given the success track record of the incumbent CEO, the owners gave him full freedom to drive the business from day one. Within six months, the incumbent CEO started implementing all his learnings from his Lever days without studying the nuances of the new company and different business environment. The result was disaster with even key managers exiting!

We call this the 'halo error'—the tendency for allowing a strong positive impression of a person, company, brand, or product in one area to positively influence one's opinion or feelings or actions in other areas. That is why we recommend an elaborate four-stage process—directing, coaching, supporting and delegating—when onboarding a senior professional in a family business; 100 per cent delegation from day one can be suicidal. Better to follow the oxymoron 'detached attachment'.

'My Sons Won't' Syndrome

A patriarch always will think 'my sons are too good and love each other and will live and manage business and family in harmony'. But as sons get married and the family grows alongside the business, complexities in both may emerge and this becomes increasingly challenging. If the two sons' profiles are different (which is bound to be the case), dilemmas and differences crop up. Even at this stage, the patriarch continues with the 'my sons won't' syndrome. Timely intervention by way of a constitution/ family charter is called for, before things go out of control.

'All by Myself'

'Nobody can fit into my shoes; I built the business from scratch', is the refrain of a business owner. While preparing a constitution, retirement age is a bone of contention with patriarchs. The question is, 'how can I retire from my own business? Till my last breath, I will manage the show'. Not letting go even in one's old age prevents GenNext from entering the business and scaling it.

These predispositions are major impediments to scaling and growth. Exposing the patriarch to other family business success stories and understanding the difference between ownership and management are the way out. Marshall Goldsmith's book on *What Got You Here Won't Get You There*, is relevant in this context.[1]

Openness to Feedback

Some family business owners are not open to critical feedback, more so from professional managers. This attitude kills professionalization of family business in the bud. Coterie formation around the patriarch is a result of surrounding yourself with only those who tell you what is sweet to your ears.

'Please All' Approach

Entering into difficult conversations with your family and team members is a challenge to be faced. The please-all approach results in mediocrity and not meeting challenges head-on. Calling a spade, a spade and being upfront on performance and governance issues are a must. If the approach continues to be 'please all', better to sell ice-cream at the beach!

Which Hat to Wear?

During a strategy session, the father as the chairman of the company (who built the business from scratch) told his daughter (the VP, Business Development) that she knew nothing about the business and not to be childish. The daughter also replied in the same tone, in the presence of a team of professional managers. Both were wearing the same hat that they wore at home—that of father and daughter. If they had the worn their official hats (chairman and VP), the conversation in front of the team wouldn't be this bad.

Expert Take by M.S.A. Kumar

'There is no sense in punishing your future for the mistakes of your past. Forgive yourself, grow from it, and then let it go,' said Melanie Koulouris.

Learning from mistakes is all about understanding what one did wrong and making sure not to repeat it. Easier said than done. I will narrate my experience when I was president of The Indus Entrepreneurs (a not-for-profit organization for fostering entrepreneurship), Kerala. While organizing a start-up conclave, we wanted to have a session on 'Failures'. It was a mammoth task to get speakers to stand up and say what all they had learnt from their mistakes and failures in the past. There is a taboo in our culture against owning up to failures. But that is changing, especially with the new generation entering the business.

Businessmen sometimes assume that if successful in one vertical and having learnt the art and science of leadership and management en route, they can succeed in any vertical. One of my friends, who was immensely successful in textile and garments vertical and amassed wealth, diversified into Real Estate. The two vastly different verticals called for unique skills and before he could realize it, he had reached bankruptcy. We recommend the

RT-PCR test before investing in new ventures (RT = return, P = potential, C = capability and R = risk).

Acknowledge mistakes, reframe and analyse the mistake, ask yourself the hard questions, put the lessons you have learnt into practice and finally remember that we can't avoid making mistakes. But learn not to repeat the same mistake.

13

OUTSIDERS AS INSIDERS

The Imperative of Family Business Advisors and Mediators

- A South Indian family business, which is into the manufacture and distribution of rubber-based products across the country, saw deep conflict among its family members. The bone of contention was the role of the chairman, who was one of the family patriarchs. Finally, in a bid to break the impasse, the group decided to invite a renowned family business advisor who was acceptable to both sides to step into the chairman's role to bring peace and stability.
- In another instance, this time in North India, an MSME group—with a manufacturing business managed by two brothers, who love each other dearly and are fiercely committed to the other—found itself in a quagmire because

of their wives and the mother. One of the wives came from a typical middle-class background following a love marriage, while the other wife belonged to a rich business family. The three ladies had huge issues in the kitchen: who would call the shots regarding the menu for the day, who would manage the servants and cooks, who would the staff report to, etc. In this milieu the mother lost about ten kilograms due to stress, while one of the brothers gained an equal amount. The conflict in the kitchen was beginning to impact the running of the business and finally they called a family business advisor to resolve the issues at home and work.

- Spiritual guru Sri Sri Ravi Shankar has a family mediation cell in his organization, the Art of Living, equipped with advisors, lawyers and consultants who try to bring peace and lasting solutions to warring families, including family businesses.
- A medium-sized export group was managed by the seventy-five-year-old chairman and his forty-two-year-old daughter in charge of business development. The chairman wanted to pass the baton on to his daughter, who is well educated and capable. The issue was that communication between the two was not of the right tone and tenor. The father wanted to ensure he passed on the mantle to his daughter after proper coaching and mentoring. Thus, the father engaged a family business advisor who is also a certified coach.
- Two co-founders were brothers-in-law. They worked together for over thirty years and built a successful organization with a top line of Rs 400 crore. The brother was street-smart and the brother-in-law was a strong technical hand with a PhD.

However, when GenNext members entered the business they became impatient with the slow pace of growth. The potential of their business vertical was huge and turnover could grow to Rs 1,000 crore within three years. However, the company's internal managerial resources lacked the bandwidth to take the company to Rs 1,000 crore. They didn't know how to go ahead with the transformation and growth of the company. The company finally hired a family business advisor who first helped them to set up the organizational structure and then define processes and systems.

After establishing the foundation, a CEO was hired from outside. This was followed by writing a family business constitution. The founders felt the need for the constitution with expected entry of GenNext. The organization is clearly on their scaling-up journey and is well-equipped thanks to the intervention of the advisor.

Why Advisors and Mediators Are Crucial

Professor Kavil Ramachandran has an interesting take on why external advisors may be useful to family businesses. He says that a lot of problems with and within family businesses are because they don't know that there is a problem. They do not realize that it is because of the unique context that they are in that they have a problem. Often, they fail to understand that business is different and family is different. Business is based on competitiveness. Family is based on compassion, relationship, adjustments, equality whereas business is merit-based. So, there are some fundamental differences between family and business and some business families do not know how to handle the interface of the two. In such situations, an advisor creates the right awareness and helps in training and counselling.

As we have seen in the preceding chapters, scaling is a challenge and can be accomplished with a raft of strategies like professionalization, going global, unlocking value and succession planning. Family constitutions need to be tailored and customized for a specific family business. Most of these are best achieved by the intervention and collaboration of family business advisors: external hands who work internally closely with the promoters and the senior leadership. Sometimes, these are short-term assignments and quite often they last for several years.

Another reason why advisors may be crucial especially in MSMEs, is that these companies by nature of their slow evolvement and small size do not have many professionals who can otherwise guide and take professional decisions. Additionally, many of the MSMEs operate in the field of manufacturing as opposed to the new-age start-ups which are mainly in the services line. Manufacturing as such attracts lesser number of professionals.

Situations of conflict within family businesses are best resolved through an independent mediator or advisor who can help take a professional, independent decision. Consider the example of two brothers who run an MSME firm. The elder brother had a strategic mind and was quick to take decisions. The younger one looked after operations and was slow to take decision calls. Their business was real-estate development, and buying of land was a crucial component in this. Real-estate brokers preferred to work with the elder brother because he took quicker decisions. The younger brother felt upset that his authority was being undermined. Anil Sainani who advises this group says that the main reason for the conflict was that roles, rules and responsibilities were not defined in the organization. As an advisor, he facilitated communication between the two brothers and set up processes and roles and helped resolve the conflict.

Family business advisors also act as a bridge between the younger and the older generations when there is conflict between the two. A trend prevalent now is that after members of the younger generation go overseas and return, they do not want to join the family business but want to start out on their own. The older generation feels that the investment in their education is wasted. In such cases, advisors come in before the children go abroad and tell them about the need and imperative to join the family business.

'Communication sensitivity' among the family members (like the father and daughter; the brothers; and the brothers-in-law mentioned earlier) is another area where family businesses seek outside help through a trusted advisor. Trust is the key word here. Many hot and sensitive matters, which the family members find difficult to communicate, are better handled by an outsider with the required tact and diplomacy. One word of caution—select an advisor with sufficient experience in handling similar situations and allow him enough time to gain the trust of all family members. We have come across instances wherein an inexperienced advisor did harm to the organization while handling family and business matters. Caution is advised here. In normal consultancy assignments, like setting up HR systems or working on a budgetary planning and control system, trust may not be that much of a key factor.

Professor Kavil Ramachandran argues that in the life-cycle of a family business many face a mid-life crisis. This crisis is driven by three different forces hitting the firm at the same time. (i) Strategy: they don't know how to grow, where to grow, and often there is no consensus on the strategy for growth. (ii) Family governance: who are the people who are involved in the business; should they all be there or not; are they clear about their roles and responsibilities, entry rules, rewards, ownership and the role of the NextGen, etc. (iii) Professionalization: following its change from a start-up to a growth firm, it has to have a clear organizational structure, well-defined and clear processes (including for decision-making), control systems, reporting systems and information systems.

Without all of the above strategy doesn't get implemented. There is then a gridlock in the company. Crises are often best resolved by outsiders who play the role of insiders.

Beyond family business advisors, who are consultants or academicians, there is a small but growing group of legal mediators who are gaining relevance and importance in the growth and maturity of family businesses. Boston- and Bangalore-based Tara Ollapally of CAMP Arbitration & Mediation is one such internationally renowned mediation practitioner who is helping a number of Indian family businesses, particularly with conflict resolution which in turn leads to sustainable solutions, and an environment of peace and growth of the business.

Varying Roles of Advisors

While family business advisors and mediators from both industry and academia perform a key role in helping companies grow, their roles are also very diverse. We briefly share the nature and scope of the work undertaken by three advisors, below.

Professor Kavil Ramachandran of ISB, Hyderabad says that he plays two roles: informal and formal. In the former, he does *pro bono* work where he does not charge any money. For instance, sometimes, family business members ask him for an hour of his time and in that hour, he might offer some potential solutions. In these instances, he acts like a family doctor who gives a broad diagnosis. In some instances, he asks for a donation to a small foundation that he has created.

In his formal role he does paid advisory work and consulting but tries to limit these cases to three or four at any given point of time. Within consulting, he works in two aspects of family business management. One is family business governance leading to the creation of a family constitution and then to its implementation. He does not get into the legal aspects, but connects them with legal experts. Guidance on governance could also involve discussions on succession planning and the role of women in the business. The other area where he brings a lot of insight into is strategy. Professor Ramachandran says this is a unique strength because of his exposure to both entrepreneurship and strategy in the pure business context. He undertakes strategy consulting, strategy training, entrepreneurship business planning and opportunity identification. Another role that he plays in consulting is more like a grandfather's role. This would include supporting a consulting project in a supervisory role, where he trains other advisors and family members.

P.M. Kumar, founder, Human Endeavour: He was invited by a senior patriarch and founder of a healthcare company to join as an advisor and partner the family and business in building family and business governance across three generations. Values, legacy and perpetuity were very important goals for the patriarch-founder. Over a three-year partnership, P.M. Kumar worked with them to craft a family business constitution. The aim was to propel institution building in this successful healthcare organization.

In another instance, he joined a family business as an overseas development consultant to help build its organization for growth in the sector. After a few years, he was invited to design a family constitution with full participation of the family members across three generations. The purpose of this initiative was to foster strong family values and relationships, build family governance and policies, strengthen corporate governance for institution building. This constitution has received international attention as a benchmark. The second version of the constitution is under finalization. After a fifteen-year-long association with them, P.M. Kumar retired as chairman of their group holding board.

P.M. Kumar was invited as advisor by four first-generation entrepreneurs, to restore leadership alignment, board roles and performance in their mid-size family business in dairy and related products. They had suffered an almost irreparable rupture of their working relationships. Business growth had stalled. They had sold their majority stake to a large, leading Indian conglomerate who appointed a CEO. The erstwhile founders, unable to change their roles from operating executives to investors, interfered with the CEO's authority. Morale plunged, as did profits.

Through a slew of interventions, such as improving the relationships between the founders; and team alignment between the company, the parent board and professionals, P.M. Kumar brought the company back to profitable growth.

Creation of family business and ownership charters is another specialization that P.M. Kumar is well known for. If the family considers, or after discussions he considers, or both of them together come to the conclusion that the business is a risk to the family and ownership, then it requires a business charter. If the family is a risk to the business and ownership, it requires a family charter. If the ownership is a risk to the family and the business, it requires an ownership charter including putting in governance structures. Only when the founder or client or the family members, particularly the senior family members, state that they want to move on to the next generation, succession, perpetuity, is there a need to have all three charters.

Anil Sainani, founder and managing partner, BAF Consultants: One of the central problems within business families, believes Anil Sainani, is that they lose the ability to communicate, and have baggage in their relationships. There is need to understand the pain of the other person, understand each other's perspectives, and understand each other's needs to resolve communication and relationship issues. Importantly, one of his key roles is to help family members regain the ability to communicate with each other. He notes that there are times when you may not agree with the other's perspective. You may agree to disagree, but wronging each other creates an emotional turmoil that makes the situation even worse. When emotionally overwrought, one cannot think, communicate or act properly.

Anil Sainani recalls a case when he was already advisor to a family business, and was consulted on issues the family faced with a prospective daughter-in-law. The family was conservative and strict vegetarians and one son wanted to marry a divorcee who was older than him and ate non-vegetarian food. Another case where his help was sought, was in family business where the son was active in the business, the daughter less active. However, she was marrying a professional and wanted her share of the family ownership to go to both of them. Could she or her husband come and work in the business?

These are typical dilemmas in family businesses that need to be addressed and resolved.

Anil Sainani also feels that the older model of the family constitution no longer provides an effective solution in present times. He advises families on creating what he calls the 'family constitution plus', which apart from laying down systems and processes also has inherent strengths and features to resolve problems on a sustainable basis. Says Sainani, 'This way of working has more credibility because if you don't live up to the document, then it self-corrects itself.'

Importance of Mediation: Tara Ollapally, Co-founder and Senior Mediator, Campmediation

Despite all the systems that family businesses might put in place, conflict is an inevitable and a normal form of relating to other people. What is important is whether the conflict is turned into a point of learning and growth; a point where business relationships and personal relationships can actually be built; a point where there could be an increased understanding of self, of the other, and the situation itself. These are issues that become points of destruction or healing, depending on the way they are managed.

Families have been stuck in court for over a decade, have destroyed each other, watched their businesses crumble, and then signed a resolution to actually come back together to rebuild those businesses. They have then found unimaginable business success, and life after conflict has been better than life before conflict.

Says Tara Ollapally, 'The mediation process, a dispute resolution process that is recognized by our legal system is very different from the court process.' She defines it as, 'A process that brings parties together, to find resolution through understanding and grow from the point of conflict.'

Once mediators step in, they use mechanisms to get the parties out of the conflict trap. Dispute resolution mechanisms are structured along a 'de-escalation ladder' to de-escalate conflict and are designed to understand and address the emotions, needs, aspirations, history, facts, and the business, legal and financial issues of all parties in the dispute.

Conflicts faced by family businesses have a dual aspect: relationship issues; and business problems. Both need to be solved. Family businesses find it particularly challenging to have sustainable long-lasting relationships. The kind of interventions family businesses bring in, their timing, and handling matters with sensitivity, are key. If such measures are not put in place, the conflict can rapidly escalate to a legal dispute. Most family businesses come to mediators over decisions that need to be made over a business problem.

Differences between mediation and the legal process: Mediation is a confidential and voluntary process in which parties make their own decisions based on an understanding of their own views, each other's views and the reality that they face. And what is the role of the mediator? The mediator works as a non-cohesive neutral, helping parties negotiate an agreement that serves them better than their alternative. It is a confidential and voluntary process.

One cannot summon the parties into mediation the way a court can summon them into the process. Parties make their decision; a mediator's decision, unlike that taken by a judge, is not binding on the parties. The mediator helps the parties make their own decision after understanding what they want, what the other party wants, and the alternative (which to a large extent, is taking the dispute to the court).

The main difference between mediation and the traditional legal process is that in mediation, the mediator works with the parties to understand the legal reality of the situation and what their alternatives are, rather than imposing a decision on them. While mediation is recognized by the legal system and can be a more formal process with specific legislation, the approach to managing disputes and using communication skills to facilitate resolution is similar in both.

Mediation in our country is largely driven by court-annexed mediation programmes. The judge refers the parties to mediation. Mediators are trying to mediate before parties go to court.

Nevertheless, the court-annexed mediation programme is a fantastic resource for dispute in the community. But it is a pro bono service. Parties cannot choose a mediator. Success depends on whether the mediator is comfortable with the issues the parties are facing, and whether she/he is skilled in the process. That is the difference between court-annexed mediation and private mediation or a private institutional mediation.

The main differences between court litigation/arbitration and mediation are:

Adversarial vs. collaborative: Litigation and arbitration are adversarial processes where parties make arguments to a neutral third party who determines right or wrong, while mediation is a collaborative process where stakeholders work together to problem-solve and find a resolution.

Role of parties and lawyers: In mediation, the parties and their lawyers play a central role in the process and decision-making, while in litigation and arbitration, the lawyers represent the parties, and the judge or arbitrator makes the decision.

Role of the neutral person/party: In litigation and arbitration, the neutral person/party plays a heavy role in determining the outcome, whereas in mediation, the neutral person/party facilitates the dispute resolution process, but the disputing parties make the final decision.

Law vs. other aspects: In litigation and arbitration, the law governs the processes, while in mediation, the law is one aspect among many that form the entire dispute.

When serving as a mediator, even if the mediator is a lawyer, they do not act as a lawyer but rather remain neutral and do not represent either party. The parties typically have their own legal experts to provide advice. However, the mediator's legal training and experience can help them better understand the legal issues and ask relevant questions. The mediator's neutrality allows them to bring the reality of the situation into the discussion more effectively, and they do not render opinions or provide legal advice. Instead, their role is to guide the parties to better understand the legal issues at hand.

The presence of lawyers during mediation is crucial because they help parties understand their legal rights and negotiate within that framework. Settlement negotiations take place against the backdrop of the law, so it's important for parties to know that their rights are being protected and that they're not giving up anything they're entitled to. Legal counsel is always brought in, depending on the complexity of the case. Parties are typically represented by their lawyers throughout the process, or lawyers are brought in as legal experts to help parties understand the law. In summary, bringing in lawyers is an essential part of the mediation process.

The mediator's role is to facilitate a negotiation using interest-based negotiation techniques. This approach seeks to understand the underlying interests and needs of each party and identify potential trade-offs and opportunities for resolution across issues. The mediator works to get the parties back to the table in a constructive way, by identifying the elements that need to be brought into the negotiation, including people, documentation, valuation, and the status of the law. This interest-based negotiation framework was developed at Harvard Law School in the 1980s and is outlined in the book *Getting to Yes*, which is considered the Bible for this approach.[1] Research shows that interest-based negotiation is more effective than the more common positional negotiation approach in achieving sustainable, long-lasting solutions.

In negotiations, mediators bring in the element of the law to help parties understand the reality of court, the time factor and the cost of litigation as part of the alternatives to the mediation process. Mediators also explore the underlying interests of a mediation—understanding why parties want what they want, such as their needs, goals, concerns, and fears. This is in contrast to the legal process, which focuses on justifying the prayer based on legal arguments.

Using professional mediators is important because they are trained in a structured yet flexible process that includes fundamental tenets such as confidentiality, voluntariness, and self-determination. They have skills, techniques, and set goals at each stage of the process, which are essential for successfully mediating conflicts.

Building trust is definitely a critical component of the mediation process. It can be a challenge to establish that trust when parties may not have experience with mediation or may not be familiar with the mediator. Education and awareness are important to help people understand the benefits of mediation and the role of the mediator. It's also important for mediators to have the skills to build trust and create a safe space for parties to discuss their concerns and interests. It sounds like a delicate balance between educating the community and building trust with the individual parties involved in each case.

Although many mediators may not have studied psychology formally, it is still an important part of mediator training. Mediators learn to understand biases and how to communicate effectively with parties in order to facilitate the resolution process. While some mediators come from psychology backgrounds, others may come from legal or other fields. In the US, the combination of psychology and law is a popular background for mediators, and many psychologists also provide mediation services. Law schools should include a course on psychology.

Mediators use their psychology knowledge to help parties in conflict to think rationally and calm their emotions by connecting to them with empathy. This helps to humanize the problem, move it from a legalistic problem to one of understanding the people in conflict and engaging them in better decision-making. Mediation is a necessary process for family businesses as it preserves relationships, is confidential and cost-effective. Seeking assisted negotiation through mediation before using the nuclear option of arbitration or litigation, is advisable.

Financial or technical experts are often brought in to help resolve disputes in mediations. However, the role of family business advisors in mediations has not yet been explored much. One potential role for family business advisors is to refer disputes to mediation and participate in the mediation process. Another potential role is to work with the mediator and parties to design a mediation process that is suited to the family business context. Additionally, family business advisors could assist in the execution of settlement terms after they are signed. Overall, the role of family business advisors in mediations is an area that requires further exploration.

The success of a mediation depends on the skill of the mediator.

There are two critical factors in successful mediation. The first is the process, which is essential in helping parties move forward. A professional mediator is skilled in this process and knows how to work with the parties to achieve resolution. The second critical factor is the mediator's ability to manage and allow emotions. High emotions are common, particularly in family businesses, and if not managed well, can derail the mediation process or lead to suboptimal outcomes. The ability to use emotions to move parties forward is a key skill of a good mediator. While negotiations are also important, the process and emotion management are the two most critical elements of successful mediation.

Post resolution, in all the several hundred cases that take place, there's only one that probably needs to go to court, in terms of the parties not complying with a settlement agreement and therefore needing to go in for enforcement.

The settlement agreement is binding only when the parties sign it. There is a pending mediation bill in Parliament which, when passed, will give a mediated settlement agreement the same validity as a court decree. Until then, the settlement agreement can be treated as a legal contract or a conciliator's settlement agreement under the Arbitration and Conciliation Act, 1996, which has the same validity as an arbitral award under section 74 of the Act. Therefore, although the legislation is pending, there are legal mechanisms currently in place to give the settlement agreement at least the same validity as an arbitral award.

Mediation is still in its early stages in India. While mediators can be accessed through court-annexed mediation programmes, a larger directory of mediators is still being established. With the upcoming mediation legislation, there will be a mediation council constituted in India that will outline the qualifications for mediators and accreditation standards, creating a better database of professional mediators. While the community of mediators is still small and young in India, it is growing.

The process of mediation is not new to Indian culture as trusted village elders used to resolve disputes in the past. However, in recent times, the traditional dispute resolution process has been replaced by the powerful village elder. Mediation brings back the concept of trusted neutral third parties who can work with parties in dispute to find their own resolution through dialogue and understanding. In the next ten to fifteen years there is likely to be a big change in the way disputes are resolved, as the current court system leads to one dispute breeding forty disputes, while the mediation process can bring together forty cases and find one resolution.

There are conflicts in family businesses, but they don't come out as nobody speaks of them openly. Business families can talk about professionalization, they can talk about succession planning, governance, writing a family constitution, etc. But when it comes to conflict people are unwilling to talk in public.

Sums up Tara Ollapally, 'Disagreements are a part of life, and it's natural to expect them. However, when two parties can no longer communicate with each other and the situation escalates, mediation becomes necessary. Especially within families, parties try to work out their issues themselves and often succeed. However, when communication breaks down and they can no longer advocate for themselves or hear the other side constructively, it's time to bring in a mediator.'

Reaching a Successful Conclusion

Despite the main successes through the intervention of family business advisors and mediators, there are challenges aplenty in their work.

In many cases business families don't wake up unless there is a crisis and then it may be too late. Second is that even if they wake up, they don't complete the journey towards a sustainable solution. Prof. Ramachandran points out that advisors/mediators are not always completely successful, because a solution depends not only on them but also on the disputing parties involved. Since family members, often carrying emotional baggage, are involved in execution, handholding by the advisor/ mediator is critical to ensure flawless implementation and to manage differences and dilemmas through powerful conversations. A lot of it is to do with whether they implement the advisor/ mediator suggestions or not.

Family business patriarchs assume their children are gems and will never fight over family wealth, business matters or management roles. Once the little gems grow up, developing their own differing personas and the clan grows larger with marriage and children, the equations change. The patriarch is oblivious to the changes in both family structure and the changing business landscape with ever-new challenges. In such a situation, Prof. Kavil Ramachandran's 5D model (dilemmas, deviations, differences, disputes and destruction) sets in.

If a family business has moved beyond disputes and is washing dirty linen in public, an advisor has a limited role to play and she/

he may be ineffective as well, if the wounds are too deep. In such a case the family has reached the decision point: keep unity or break up amicably. If the latter seems the only option the family business advisor has to give way to accountants and lawyers.

Building trust between disputing parties requires a lot of time, before the actual resolution process starts. It is what is called chemistry mapping. There are a number of meetings talking about this and that till the satisfaction level reaches a point where both are capable of being trustworthy to each other.

Many family members who are engaged in this process might feel that because one relative was contacted before another, or if one relative is anchoring the project, they person might be favoured. But there is no beneficial treatment. This is no individual work. Generally, there is an anchor. Nowadays the second and third generation, not the founder, are taking on the anchor's role. But it doesn't mean the anchor is the representative for the founder. After signing on with an advisor, the entire family is on one side, irrespective of individuals, and definitely the organization on the other side is the central point of focus.

There are three ways in which a client can work with an advisor: the client knows what he wants; builds a patient-doctor relationship; or develops a partner relationship. Most importantly, it is important for the two of them to develop mutual trust. That is the touchstone of the success barometer. In the final analysis, the benefits of bringing in a family business advisor outweigh the challenges that may be faced. More often than not, the family members gain in confidence, conflicts are resolved, sustainable solutions are found and the business goes on to scale and grow.

Expert Take by M.S.A. Kumar

I was approached by a family business owner who wanted a written constitution/code of conduct. Within two meetings, I came to the conclusion that a constitution would not serve much purpose as there were multiple leaders in the business with no clearly defined roles. Disagreements were galore with delayed decision-making, as there was no one leader running the show. The business sank to new lows.

As P.M. Kumar mentions, in this case, the business was put at risk due to family and ownership issues. Therefore, the prioritized need was to get a business charter in place with a well-defined organizational structure, clearly defined roles and responsibilities for all including founders and professional managers, and performance review systems.

My recommendation of a business charter wasn't acceptable to the owner and I had to walk out of the assignment. The need of the business has to be ascertained first and family business owners should enter the advisory process with an open and flexible mind.

Given the handholding role of an advisor during the execution/ implementation stage, the tenure of the engagement may have to be extended to get maximum impact from the engagement. While deciding on an advisor, the family business owner should discuss the matter with other family members and arrive at a 'needs chart'. This chart will help evaluate the advisor's capability to fulfil those needs.

More importantly, the family must assess the advisor's cultural fit with the family. The family must also allow some time for mutual building of trust and factor that in the engagement contract. A good advisor will always factor-in this trust-building period, in the time needed.

For scaling and building a family business that lasts beyond three generations, build an entrepreneurial pipeline in the family (to encourage family members to start new businesses, instead of crowding the existing business), and a leadership pipeline consisting of both family and non-family members.

Building a family business that lasts beyond three generations is not easy. But as we have shown in this book, it is possible. It is important to do so not only for family businesses, but the Indian economy and the nation as a whole.

EPILOGUE

Summing Up: The 7Cs

IN CHAPTER 12 WE DELIBERATED ON 'WHAT NOT TO DO: Learning from Mistakes'. In this epilogue, we attempt to synthesize the twelve case studies on what these businesses did right, and learning from these right actions and decisions.

There are some common threads cutting across the cases which will be the key takeaways from this book.

In the preceding thirteen chapters we covered twelve family-business case studies: Aravind Eye Care System (Madurai); Bhima Jewellers (Kochi); Dodla Dairy (Hyderabad); Eastern Condiments and Group Meeran (Kochi); ELICO Ltd (Hyderabad); Evolve Back (Orange County Resorts & Hotels; Bengaluru); Gera Developments (Pune); House of Anita Dongre (Mumbai); IBS Software (Kochi and Singapore); OmniActive

Health Technologies of the Sanjaya Mariwala Group (Mumbai); Popular Automobiles (Kochi); and Sandu Pharmaceuticals (Mumbai).

Though the twelve family-managed enterprises are from different manufacturing and service verticals, diverse geographies, different sizes (within MSME definition) and varying family sizes and backgrounds, there are common threads weaving the twelve case studies, which are summed up in the '7Cs' framework: clarity, commitment, consistency, courage, cohesion, competency and compounding for scaling-up.

Clarity: The mind drives and dictates actions. Therefore, clarity of thought is a prerequisite to growth and transformation of family businesses—be it clarity of purpose, or of strategy, or of roles and responsibilities. Delegation will not happen unless there is clarity in roles and responsibilities across the organization. Navas Meeran of Eastern Condiments was clear in his mind about growth beyond Kerala. Realizing that depending on family funds wouldn't be sufficient to realize his goal, he reached out to private equity for funding. Same is the case with Jose Ramapuram of Evolve Back Resorts. Positioning the product at the top, super-luxury segment was part of the family's DNA. Clarity of mind again played a role here in all actions following this thought. Evolve Back thus developed a ten-point blueprint for all its employees, in line with the super luxury brand positioning mentioned in Chapter 8. The ten-point blueprint thus became values for Evolve Back—accepted ways of employee behaviour to achieve customer delight and building the brand.

Commitment: Single-minded focus results in committing to a purpose of the business and goals to accomplish. Commitment extends to all the stakeholders, be it employees, customers, shareholders and society at large. IBS Software founder V.K. Mathews ensured the company had single-minded focus on a single sector: travel (aviation and shipping) and tourism. He resisted the huge temptation to have a diversified portfolio and this commitment resulted in IBS Software scaling up from 55 employees when they started in 1997 from a single location in Trivandrum, to over 3,500 employees from 40 nationalities with operations in 40 countries today. Businesses have multiple stakeholders and the leaders make commitments to the stakeholders. Keeping up the commitments to all stakeholders calls for tact and a tight balancing act.

Consistency: This is a key attribute to build a family business institution going beyond three generations. Many family businesses build consistency in their ethos through a set of values both in family and business. One such value seen across all the twelve cases is placing the organization above self, which has ensured growth and minimized conflicts. Another key element of consistency is having a long-term vision (where you want to go) and a well-stated mission (why are we in this business; defining the core purpose). Thus building an institution that goes beyond three generations starts with having a workshop on 'vision, mission and values' for all family members (whether active in business or not) along with the senior management team. This workshop ensures alignment amongst family members and the top management team and builds-in the consistency element.

Courage: Entrepreneurship is the ability to go beyond what is ordinary and already exists. Directly related to one's risk-taking ability, courage is the key element in decision-making.

Depending on only family members for scaling-up instead of hiring professionals is an exhibition of lack of courage and willingness to trust and delegate to outside professionals. This hampers growth and scaling-up and another reason why family businesses don't go beyond three generations. Learning from the example of Gera Developments—starting as refugees of partition in 1947, they have today built sixty-two projects and approximately 6 million square feet of development, winning the trust of 8,000+ customers with projects in Pune, Goa and Bengaluru.

Cohesion: A must-have attribute for family businesses to scale-up, grow and transform is cohesion among family members, apart from cohesion between management team and family members. Here, the role of the family business patriarch or matriarch is very crucial. Conflicts among family members can't be wished away; one has to take it as normal. Managing the conflicts and finding working solutions is the role of the head of the family. That results in cohesion. Take the case of Evolve Back. Thomas E. Ramapuram and his seven sons built the business from scratch and the sons continue to stay together even today. The Ramapuram family decided to write a family constitution, outlining the dos and don'ts. That may be another reason for their cohesion, though we are of the opinion that family constitution is not a must for all family businesses. The fact is that a family constitution minimizes the conflicts resulting in better cohesion.

Competency: The late C.K. Prahalad brought in the concept of 'core competency'. Here we are referring to a larger area of competency, which includes the intangibles like capabilities. Some family business owners think that they can do everything and manage the business. This is not erroneous thinking at the start of the business. But as the business grows, the owners may neither possess the competencies required nor have the time to look after all aspects of the business. Therefore, capability and capacity-building through professionalization is called for. All the twelve case-studies in this book have professionalized at different stages of the business life-cycle.

Compounding for scaling-up: A major challenge faced by small and medium family businesses is the ability to scale-up, grow and transform. Moving from one orbit to another in an enterprise is challenging and calls for specialized skills in transition management. The organization needs additional energy to do so. The compounding impact is very pronounced in the twelve cases and has made them successful. The previous six Cs (clarity, commitment, consistency, courage, cohesion and competency) work with synergistic effect, with each C supporting the other; there is a lot of inter-dependability.

This book hopes to have provided you with a deeper understanding of the six Cs that undergird a successful family business enterprise (clarity, commitment, consistency, courage, cohesion and competency), enabling it to compound for scaling-up (the seventh C) and thus take the business beyond three generations.

NOTES

Scan this QR code to access the detailed notes

INDEX

INDEX

INDEX

INDEX

INDEX

INDEX

INDEX

INDEX

INDEX

ABOUT THE AUTHORS

Navas Meeran is the chairman at Group Meeran, ME Meeran Foundation, president of the Kerala Football Association and former chairman of the Confederation of Indian Industry (CII), Southern Region.

Firoz Meeran is the vice chairman of Group Meeran, ME Meeran Foundation. He heads the family office of Group Meeran and is also the managing director of Scoreline Sports.

M.S.A. Kumar is family business advisor and CEO coach bringing his expertise of managing family dynamics when scaling up. An alumnus of IIM, Ahmedabad, he has worked for over four decades in senior positions in multinationals, such as Sandoz and Bayer, and family-managed businesses, such as the AV Thomas group.

ABOUT THE AUTHORS

George Skaria is a senior journalist, communications specialist and author. He has been an editor with *Businessworld, Business Today, Financial Express* and *Business Standard*, where he edited two management magazines, *Indian Management* and *Asian Management Review*. He has written for more than twenty publications in India and overseas. This is his fourth book. He lives in New Delhi.

HarperCollins *Publishers* India

At HarperCollins India, we believe in telling the best stories and finding the widest readership for our books in every format possible. We started publishing in 1992; a great deal has changed since then, but what has remained constant is the passion with which our authors write their books, the love with which readers receive them, and the sheer joy and excitement that we as publishers feel in being a part of the publishing process.

Over the years, we've had the pleasure of publishing some of the finest writing from the subcontinent and around the world, including several award-winning titles and some of the biggest bestsellers in India's publishing history. But nothing has meant more to us than the fact that millions of people have read the books we published, and that somewhere, a book of ours might have made a difference.

As we look to the future, we go back to that one word—a word which has been a driving force for us all these years.

Read.

Harper Collins

4th

HARPER PERENNIAL

HARPER BUSINESS

HARPER BLACK

हार्पर हिन्दी

HarperCollins *Children's Books*

HARPER DESIGN

HARPER VANTAGE

Harper Sport